The People Behind Deadly TERRORIST ATTACKS

Laura La Bella

E **Enslow Publishing**
101 W. 23rd Street
Suite 240
New York, NY 10011
USA

enslow.com

Published in 2017 by Enslow Publishing, LLC.
101 W. 23rd Street, Suite 240, New York, NY 10011

Library of Congress Cataloging-in-Publication Data
Names: La Bella, Laura, author.
Title: The people behind deadly terrorist attacks / Laura La Bella.
Description: New York, NY : Enslow Publishing, 2017. | Series: The psychology of mass murderers | Includes bibliographical references and index.
Identifiers: LCCN 2016010538 | ISBN 9780766077751 (library bound)
Subjects: LCSH: Terrorism—Juvenile literature. | Terrorists—Juvenile literature.
Classification: LCC HV6431 .L224 2017 | DDC 363.325—dc23
LC record available at https://lccn.loc.gov/2016010538

Printed in the United States of America

To Our Readers: We have done our best to make sure all websites in this book were active and appropriate when we went to press. However, the author and the publisher have no control over and assume no liability for the material available on those websites or on any websites they may link to. Any comments or suggestions can be sent by e-mail to customerservice@enslow.com.

Photo Credits: Cover, pp. 1, 60, 108 © AP Images; throughout book, chrupka/Shutterstock.com (scratched black background); Merkushev Vasiliy/Shutterstock.com (red background), Tiberiu Stan/Shutterstock.com (brain waves); p. 6 JACQUES DEMARTHON/AFP/Getty Images; p. 14 Getty Images News/Getty Images; p. 16 Tammy KLEIN/Gamma-Rapho/Getty Images; p. 19 Handout/Getty Images News/Getty Images; p. 20 Joe Raedle/Getty Images News/Getty Images; pp. 21, 25 Erick S. Letter/Stringer/Getty Images News/Getty Images; p. 27 Thomas Cooper/Stringer/Getty Images News; p. 28 Arapahoe County Sheriff's Office via Getty Images/Handout/Getty Images News; p. 32 Connecticut State Police via Getty Images/Handout/Getty Images News; p. 33 Anthony Behar/Barcroft Media via Getty Images; p. 36 Kevin Moloney/Hulton Archive/Getty Images; p. 37 MARK LEFFINGWELL/AFP/Getty Images; p. 38 Marc Piscotty/Stringer/Getty Images News/Getty Images; p. 41 Kevin C. Cox/Getty Images News; p. 44 DAVIS TURNER/AFP/Getty Images; p. 45 Jahi Chikwendiu-Pool/Getty Images News/Getty Images; p. 49 Getty Images News/Stringer/Getty Images; pp. 52, 54 BOB DAEMMERICH/AFP/Getty Images; p. 56 POOL PHOT/AFP/Getty Images; p. 65 William F. Campbell/The LIFE Images Collection/Getty Images; p. 67 Charleston Country Sheriff's Office via Getty Images News/Handout/Getty Images; p. 68 Winn McNamee/Getty Images; p. 71 FBI via Getty Images/Handout/Getty Images News; p. 73 Scott Olson/Getty Images News/Getty Images; p. 76 CHRIS KLEPONIS/AFP/Getty Images; p. 80 Angel Valentin/Getty Images News/Getty Images; p. 81 Susana Gonzalez/Bloomberg/Getty Images; p. 84 Eric VANDEVILLE/Gamme-Rapho/Getty Images; p. 89 CHRISTOPHE SIMON/AFP/Getty Images; p. 93 Julio Cesar Aguilar/AFP/Getty Images; p. 97 The Asahi Shimbun via Getty Images; p. 102 Andrew Harrer/Bloomberg/Getty Images; p. 105 ROBYN BECK/AFP/Getty Images; p. 108 Gustavo Caballero/Getty Images Entertainment/Getty Images.

Contents

Seeks revenge. In 30 percent of mass killings, family members are the main victims. The next most likely target is the workplace, to take revenge on a boss or coworkers. Some mass murderers blame society and open fire in public places, or they target police.

Has access to high-powered weapons. Daniel Nagin, a criminologist at Carnegie Mellon University, says, "It's technologically impossible to kill a lot of people very quickly without access to assault weapons."

Blames other people for his or her problems.

Often has a mental illness, particularly paranoid schizophrenia.

Is a loner, with few friends or social connections.

Carefully plans the attacks, taking days to months to get ready.

Has suicidal tendencies.

Has made violent threats, to the target or others indirectly, prior to the attack.

Is often reacting to a stressor just prior to the rampage, such as the loss of a job or a relationship.

The actions are not often a surprise to those who know him or her.

INTRODUCTION

On the evening of November 13, 2015, supporters of ISIS, the Islamic State of Iraq and the Levant, an Islamic extremist group that promotes religious violence through terrorist activities, coordinated a series of attacks in Paris, France, that killed 130 people and injured another 368. Over the course of the night, suicide bombers and armed gunmen terrorized cafés, restaurants, and a popular music venue.

Friends of Dylann Roof, a twenty-one-year-old who allegedly murdered nine people at a church in South Carolina, told investigators that Roof wanted to start a race war when he attended a prayer meeting at Emanuel African Methodist Episcopal Church, a historic black church in Charleston. Roof arrived at the church and spent an hour participating in a Bible study group before he allegedly opened fire and killed seven parishioners.

These acts of violence were designed by their perpetrators to cause fear, intimidation, and death. Terrorism can trace its history back to the French Revolution, when it was developed as a form of warfare. But the most widely accepted and more modern definition of the word finds terrorism connected most strongly to politics and power.[2] Terrorists use violence in the pursuit of power that can lead to social or political change. Terrorism includes not only acts of violence but also the threat of violence. Often, terrorists use threats to coerce people, organizations, or governments into doing something the terrorist(s) wants.

Terrorist attacks and events, and the physical and psychological violence associated with it, are committed by both groups and organizations, and by individuals acting alone. And each act of

US Secretary of Defense Ashton Carter and US ambassador to France Jane D. Hartley pay tribute to the victims of the 2015 Paris terror attacks at the Place de la Republique (Republic Square) on January 20, 2016.

terror is fueled by its own set of motivations, whether it's to draw attention to a cause or belief, to enact political change, to influence a government, or to instill widespread fear, uncertainty, and intimidation.

There are different types of terrorism—religious terrorism, pathological terrorism, issue-oriented terrorism, political terrorism, narcotics-based terrorism, and cyberterrorism—each categorized by the type of place the terrorists decide to attack and its overall goal. Some terrorism attacks are designed to shock the world. Others have the sole purpose of hurting or killing as many people as possible, while other attacks are used to draw attention to an issue or to make a political statement. Some attacks purposefully target controversial sites or culturally sensitive locations, such as acts against abortion clinics and churches. Some acts are solely intended to create fear and uncertainty, such as school shootings. Others are planned to disrupt government proceedings or a country's financial stability. These attacks happen at government buildings or at centers of financial activity. High-tech cyberattacks steal personal data, government plans, or sensitive military information.

Terrorist activities can include bombings, kidnappings, taking hostages, armed attacks, assassinations, hijackings, mass shootings, and computer hacking. The causes and motivations for terrorism can range widely, as can the types of attacks and the methods used during an incident. In general, causes and motivations can include:

- Producing widespread fear
- Obtaining attention for a cause through media coverage of an attack

- Harassing, weakening, or embarrassing a nation's security forces so that the nation's government overreacts and appears repressive
- Stealing or extorting money and equipment, especially weapons and ammunition vital to the operation of a terrorist group
- Destroying facilities or disrupting lines of communication to create doubt that the government can provide for and protect its citizens
- Discouraging foreign investments, tourism, or assistance programs that can affect the target country's economy and support of the government in power
- Influencing government decisions, legislation, or other critical decisions
- Freeing prisoners held by another country or by a specific group
- Satisfying a vengeance against a group or government

Terrorism occurs around the world, though there are hot spots where terrorism activity happens more frequently. But even these are dynamic and can change based on a variety of factors that can include conflicting views on religion or an increase in religious extremism, foreign involvement in local or regional conflicts, and emerging extremist groups with global political agendas.

Chapter 1

Religious Terrorism:
KILLING FOR GOD AND COUNTRY

The deadliest terrorist attack on American soil occurred on September 11, 2001, when nineteen terrorists from al-Qaeda, an international Islamic extremist group, hijacked four different commercial airplanes. They crashed two planes into the north and south towers of the World Trade Center in New York City, and a third into the side of the Pentagon in Washington, DC. The fourth plane crashed in a Pennsylvania field after passengers attempted to take back control of the airliner. The attacks killed 2,977 people.[1]

Al-Qaeda targeted the World Trade Center, an epicenter for global finance, and the Pentagon, the headquarters of the US Department of Defense, in hopes of weakening the United States' standing in the world and damage the nation's economy.[2] An extremist religious organization, al-Qaeda's goal was to overthrow the US government in support of radical Islam.

What Is Religious Terrorism?

Religious terrorism occurs when members of a religious-based organization use an extreme interpretation of their spiritual beliefs as motivation to attack other groups, governments, or individuals.[3] Religious terrorists and violent extremists often interpret violence or other messages of control and domination within their religion's belief structure as justification for violence, violent acts, and terrorism. These violent extremists do not represent the mainstream beliefs of their religion.

Islamic extremists are an example of a group of people who use their religion as validation for violence. Islamic extremism, also called radical Islam and Islamic supremacy, is defined by a very specific interpretation of Islam, which believes that Islamic law, or Sharia, is an all-encompassing religious-political system that should be enforced by its followers worldwide to create one Islamic state. Islamic radicals do not believe in democracy and they reject human rights.

No single religious group is more prominent than any other in committing terrorist acts. Members of nearly all of the world's major religions—including Buddhism, Christianity, Hinduism, Judaism, Islam, and Sikhism—have engaged in terrorist activities in recent history.

In recent years, since the 9/11 terrorist attacks, religious extremism has become the main force of terrorism worldwide. Of the total number of deaths across the world that can be attributed to terrorism, 80 percent have occurred in five countries: Iraq, Afghanistan, Pakistan, Nigeria, and Syria.[4] These five nations are known hotbeds for religious unrest, radical religious viewpoints, and conflicting religious ideologies.

Causes and Motivations for Religious Terrorism

Religious terrorism can be motivated by religious ideologies and grievances. It is a particularly dangerous form of terrorism because of the fanaticism of those who practice it and their willingness to sacrifice themselves for the cause. However, religion alone is not the sole cause of religious terrorism. Religion is among a list of factors that includes politics, culture, theological beliefs, and psychology that can influence a person or a group to target others in the name of religion.[5]

Religious terrorist organizations recruit and radicalize their members. According to a study by Pennsylvania State University's International Center for the Study of Terrorism, people who are more open to terrorist recruitment and radicalization tend to feel angry, alienated, or disenfranchised; believe they do not have the power to effect real change in the current political system; identify with perceived victims of the social injustice they want to fight; believe that violence is not immoral; are supported by friends or family; and seek a sense of identity and belonging that a group or organization can fulfill.[6]

Religious extremism—which can be defined as the acts of a person or group who holds an extreme position that if others do not follow their religion they should be punished—has become the main motivator of terrorism since the 9/11 attacks, according to the Global Peace Index, an annual survey conducted by the Institute for Economics & Peace.[7] The survey reports that out of nine geographical regions, five have become less peaceful, with the Middle East and North Africa leading the list. This is due to a rise in Islamic extremist groups.

Who Commits Religious Terrorism?

Terrorists who are motivated by their religion view the violent acts they commit as a form of spirituality, and use their terrorist activity as a way to carry out a greater purpose they view as being supported by their religion. Religious terrorists act in the name of their divine being, and often give their life to the cause. They often die acting as a suicide bomber or as a victim of their own terrorist acts. *Psychology Today* magazine cites a series of studies on the psychological impact of considering an activity to be sacred. The studies found that those who label something as sacred place a higher priority on it and derive more meaning from it than those they consider to be less sacred. Religious terrorists are more likely to use "all in" tactics, such as suicide bombings, that are supported by religious teachings used to justify, encourage, and even reward this kind of self-sacrifice in the afterlife.

What distinguishes religious terrorism from other types of terrorism is that its victims are chosen at random and are seen by terrorists as representatives of the enemy. Their enemy can be a religion, a country, or a way of life. The victims of religious terrorism are rarely, if ever, involved in the actual conflict themselves.[8]

Osama bin Laden

Born: 1957

Occupation: Leader of al-Qaeda, an extreme terrorist organization

Diagnosis: Malignant narcissism

Died: May 1, 2011

Osama bin Laden was born in Riyadh, Saudi Arabia, in 1957. He was the seventeenth of fifty-two children. Bin Laden grew up wealthy. His father, Mohammed bin Laden, owned the largest construction company in Saudi Arabia. Mohammed bin Laden died in a plane crash when Osama bin Laden was ten years old. While many of his brothers and sisters were educated at universities in the West, with several establishing residency in the United States and throughout Europe, bin Laden attended college in Jiddah, Saudi Arabia, where he earned a degree in public administration from King Adbul Aziz University. While in college, bin Laden joined the Muslim Brotherhood and soon became a follower of Abdullah Azzam, a radical pan-Islamist scholar who believed that all Muslims should rise up in jihad, or holy war, to create a single Islamic state. As bin Laden's resentment toward Westerrn influence grew, the idea of inciting a holy war appealed to him, and he grew more and more interested in radical Islam and jihad.

Osama bin Laden was the leader of the al-Qaeda terrorist group.

RELIGIOUS TERRORISM: KILLING FOR GOD AND COUNTRY

Azzam and bin Laden soon established the Maktab al-Khidamat, a global recruitment network with offices around the world, including several in the United States. The organization encouraged young Muslim men to join the Afghan jihad and provided training and supplies to further spread pan-Islamism throughout the world.[9]

Bin Laden, with support from other followers, soon established a new organization, named al-Qaeda. This terrorist group focused on carrying out symbolic acts of terrorism against the United States, its military, and its economic interests.

Through bin Laden's leadership, al Qaeda's choice of violence included bombings, assassination attempts, hijacking, kidnapping, and suicide attacks. He led his first attack, in 1991, on a hotel in Aden, Yemen, that was housing American troops who were traveling on a peacekeeping mission to Somalia, Africa. A bomb detonated, killing two tourists, but no American soldiers. He continued planning and executing attacks, including the first attack on the World Trade Center in New York City in 1993. Members of al-Qaeda parked a truck packed with explosives in the parking garage underneath the north tower. When it detonated, the bomb killed six people and injured more than one thousand.[10] The bomb also knocked out the electrical system in the tower, making evacuations difficult.

Additional terrorist attacks followed, including the bombings of two US embassies in Nairobi, Kenya, and Dar-es-Salaam, Tanzania, and the bombing of the USS *Cole*, a US Navy destroyer docked off the coast of Yemen. This attack killed seventeen servicemen serving on the ship. But on September 11, 2001, bin Laden led the deadliest attack yet on American lives.

On the morning of September 11, nineteen al-Qaeda operatives hijacked four commercial airliners, two from Logan International Airport in Boston, Massachusetts, one from Dulles International Airport in Washington, DC, and one from Newark International Airport in New Jersey. At 8:46 a.m., the first plane hit the north tower of the World Trade Center. At 9:03 a.m., a second plane hit the south tower. At 9:37 a.m., a third plane crashed into the side of the Pentagon in Washington, DC. At 10:03 a.m., the fourth plane crashed into a field in Pennsylvania after passengers fought al-Qaeda members for control of the plane. By 10:30 a.m. that morning, both towers collapsed, the side of the Pentagon lay in rubble, and a field in Pennsylvania remained engulfed in flames for hours.[11]

Terrorists hijacked two planes and crashed them into New York City's World Trade Center towers on September 11, 2001.

RELIGIOUS TERRORISM: KILLING FOR GOD AND COUNTRY

On May 1, 2011, bin Laden was killed by US Special Forces during an early morning raid on a compound in Abbottabad, Pakistan, where he had been hiding.

Osama bin Laden was never officially analyzed by trained clinicians; however, using known information about his behavior, documented attitudes, decision-making abilities and personality traits, many psychologists and professional criminal profilers from the Central Intelligence Agency have suggested a diagnosis of malignant narcissist. This condition is characterized by pathological narcissism, antisocial behavior, paranoid traits and behavior, and destructive aggression.[12]

Pattern of crime:

Bombings, assassination attempts, hijacking, kidnapping, and suicide attacks

Number of victims:

2,977 victims of the 9/11 terrorists attacks; countless other victims of additional attacks throughout al-Qaeda's history

Born: September 8, 1970
Occupation: Army psychiatrist
Arrested: November 5, 2009

Nidal Hasan was born to Palestinian immigrants who ran a restaurant and convenience store in Virginia. He graduated from Virginia Polytechnic Institute and State University and earned his doctorate in psychiatry at the Uniformed Services University of Health Sciences in 2003. During his residency and early military career, his superiors continued to promote him despite concerns over his behavior that had led many to think he had become an Islamic radical who had the potential to become a violent Islamic extremist. On more than one occasion, Hasan publicly stated that the war on terror was really a war against Islam. He even gave a public presentation on the value of suicide bombings.

Despite these concerns and questionable behavior, Hasan continued to work at Fort Hood, the largest active-duty military base, as a psychiatrist. He also continued to earn promotions, rising in rank. He treated soldiers returning from war for post-traumatic stress disorder. On November 5, 2009, Hasan went to a processing center at Fort Hood, where soldiers were preparing for deployment to overseas locations. Wearing a combat uniform, Hasan opened fire on a crowded waiting area. Several witnesses described hearing

Hasan yell "Allahu Akbar," an Arabic expression that means "God is great" prior to the shooting. Hasan fired more than two hundred rounds of ammunition before being shot by a civilian police officer. He killed thirteen people and injured thirty-two others. Hasan was left paralyzed from the waist down from injuries he sustained in the shooting.

Hasan was arrested and faced thirteen counts of premeditated murder and thirty-two counts of premeditated attempted murder.[13] He acted as his own attorney at the trial, admitted he was the shooter during his opening statement, called no witnesses during the trial, and presented very little evidence. He admitted to

US Major Nidal Hasan, an army psychiatrist, was found guilty of murder in the Fort Hood shootings.

killing soldiers to help protect the Taliban, a terrorist group based in the Middle East, and other followers of radical Islam. He made no closing statement. On August 23, 2013, a jury found Hasan guilty of forty-five counts of premeditated murder and attempted premeditated murder. He was later sentenced to death.

The shooting at Fort Hood was the sole attack committed by Hasan. According to prosecutors, Hasan spent months planning the attack. During the trial, Colonel Steve Henricks described how Hasan stockpiled bullets, practiced at a shooting range, and bought an extender kit so his pistol could hold more bullets.[14]

Army soldiers stand together as they pray during the memorial service in honor of the thirteen victims of the shooting rampage.

In the months prior to the Fort Hood shooting, US intelligence agencies, including the Federal Bureau of Investigation, intercepted up to twenty messages between Hasan and Anwar Al-Awlaki, a one-time spiritual leader at a mosque in Virginia where Hasan had once worshipped. Al-Awlaki was already known to US intelligence agencies as a high-profile American member of al-Qaeda. The investigation was part of an unrelated issue and its results were found to be consistent with a research project Hasan was conducting at Walter Reed Medical Center. Their investigation resulted in a report that stated that Hasan was not involved in any terrorist activities or terrorist planning. However, Al-Awlaki was known to have radical views, and in the aftermath of the shootings Al-Awlaki praised Hasan on his website, saying he "did the right thing" in attacking soldiers who were preparing to deploy to the Middle East." [15]

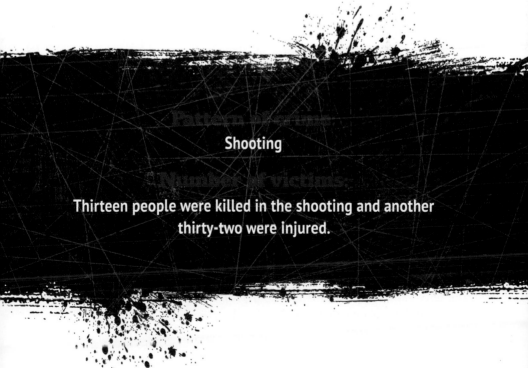

Pattern of crime

Shooting

Number of victims:

Thirteen people were killed in the shooting and another thirty-two were injured.

Born: September 19, 1966

Occupation: Specialist in the US Army

Arrested: May 31, 2003

Eric Rudolph was born in Merritt Island, Florida. His father died when Rudolph was fifteen. He moved around with his mother and siblings before he dropped out of high school. He spent time at the Church of Israel, a "Christian Identity" compound where he began to follow the anti-semitic, white-supremacy group's main beliefs: that white men are descendants of Adam and are the chosen people of God, Jews are descendants of Satan and are evil, the government cannot be trusted, and the medical profession is Jewish and doctors and medical care should be avoided.[16] After enlisting in the US Army, Rudolph was discharged after less than two years of service for substance abuse.

On July 27, 1996, during the Summer Olympic Games in Atlanta, Georgia, Rudolph arrived at Centennial Olympic Park, an area considered to be the town square of the Olympic gaming venues. During a late night concert at the park, Rudolph planted a backpack filled with pipe bombs and nails beneath a bench. A security guard noticed the backpack and alerted authorities. As law enforcement was clearing the area, the bomb detonated, killing one and injuring more than a hundred people. A second person died from a heart attack.

Bombing suspect Eric Robert Rudolph is led to his hearing in federal court on June 2, 2003.

Rudolph committed three more attacks. His pattern of attack was bombings, skills he learned in the military at Air Assault School. On January 19, 1997, two bombs exploded at a suburban Atlanta abortion clinic. Seven people were injured. One month later, on February 21, 1997, a bomb exploded at the Otherside Lounge, a gay club in Atlanta, injuring four people. On January 29, 1998, Rudolph detonated a bomb at a women's clinic in Birmingham, Alabama, killing two people and injuring one.

It wasn't until the fourth attack that investigators began to focus on Rudolph as a suspect after witnesses at a women's clinic reported seeing Rudolph walking away from a bombing. The witnesses provided police with a license plate number. Around the same time, news agencies began receiving letters claiming the Army of God, an extremist religious organization, was responsible for the two women's clinic bombings.

With evidence mounting against him, Rudolph went into hiding. The FBI and other law enforcement agencies launched searches of nearby forests. He was finally arrested when a police officer saw a man, later identified as Rudolph, rummaging through garbage behind a store. After nearly five years as a fugitive, he was captured on May 31, 2003.

Rudolph stood trial twice, first for the bombing of the women's clinic in Alabama, which claimed two lives, and a second time for the Olympic Park bombing. He faced a total of twenty-three counts related to four separate terrorist bombings. To avoid the death penalty, Rudolph agreed to plead guilty to all of the counts against him. He received four life sentences, all without parole.[17] In interviews with law enforcement, Rudolph told investigators that his anti-abortion and anti-homosexuality views motivated his attacks.

The latest specials, Captured Cappuccino and At Last Latte, appear on a coffee shop sign after the long-awaited arrest of Eric Robert Rudolph.

On the Army of God website, Rudolph wrote that the purpose of the Olympic bombing was to "confound, anger, and embarrass the Washington government in the eyes of the world for its abominable sanctioning of abortion on demand."[18] He wanted to force the cancellation of the Olympic Games to damage the financial profit of the games for both the US government and for the corporations who sponsored the event.

Pattern of crime

Bombings

Number of victims:

Four people were killed and 150 were injured.

Chapter 2

Pathological Terrorism:
INFLICTING FEAR AND TERROR

It was the opening night of *The Dark Knight Rises*, the third and final movie in the highly anticipated Batman trilogy. James Holmes entered a packed midnight showing in a Colorado movie theater and opened fire on an unsuspecting audience of moviegoers. By the time he was detained, Holmes had killed twelve people and injured more than seventy. In a notebook, recovered by investigators after the shooting, Holmes detailed his obsession with killing. For years he thought about how to kill a large number of people. He wrote passages where he fantasized about using nuclear bombs or a biological weapon to carry out a massacre. In diary entries closer to the date of the shooting, he created detailed analysis of the movie theater, outlined

James Holmes attacked moviegoers at the Century 16 movie theater during an early-morning screening of *The Dark Knight Rises*.

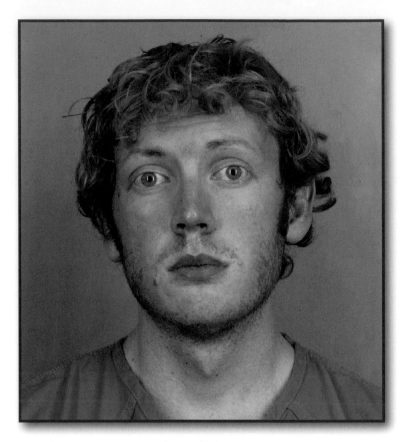

James Holmes

the location of exit doors, and documented his research into which theater had the most seats for the maximum number of casualties.[1]

What Is Pathological Terrorism?

Holmes is a pathological terrorist, an individual who utilizes various killing strategies for the sheer joy of terrorizing others.[2] Pathological terrorists often operate alone instead of within or with support from an organization or group. They often lack a well-defined motive and rarely kill in the name of religion or politics. Many pathological terrorists suffer from some form of mental illness. Pathological terrorism is most commonly carried out through school shootings and serial killing scenarios.

Who Commits Pathological Terrorism and Why

Many of the perpetrators of pathological terrorism have a history with mental illness, have committed petty crimes, have experimented with drugs, and/or have developed a sudden and extreme anti-authority ideology in which they seek to buck the rules and social norms forced upon them.[3] The individuals who have a documented or suspected mental illness often struggle to give a shape to the dark impulses that permeate their thoughts. They can be obsessive compulsive in personality or experience an alternate reality in which their actions do not carry the same emotional impact they do for those without a mental instability.

While researchers and criminologists both agree that there is no single profile for a pathological killer, they do cite anger, rage, and feelings of resentment and embitterment as influencing factors.[4] Every day, there are people who face feelings of disappointment, frustration, rage, and anger as they go about their lives. Dealings with coworkers and supervisors, interaction with government officials, disagreements between family members, even being cut off by a fellow driver on the freeway can produce intense feelings of fury, irritation, and annoyance. But the average person does not react to these feelings in extremely violent ways.

However, those who resort to mass murder and carry out large-scale shootings experience extreme levels of anger and hate that are excessive, destructive, abnormal, and out of control.

Psychologists don't believe these perpetrators simply snap one day and decide to randomly kill innocent people. Instead, they believe these feelings of anger and rage simmer slowly under the surface for months or even years. It is believed that self-control, or the ability to control one's emotions, behavior, and desires, is the key to a well-functioning life. And a lack of self-control might be the reason that some people act upon their feelings of anger, hate, and rage.

Scientific American conducted an interview with Marco Iacoboni, a University of California, Los Angeles, professor of psychiatry and biobehavioral sciences and director of the school's Transcranial Magnetic Stimulation Laboratory. They asked him why some individuals act on their violent thoughts when others do not. He explains that most people can control their actions to the extent that relatively few of the daily negative interactions they experience end in violence. But for those who resort to violence, it can come down to a person lacking the cognitive control mechanisms, or the ability to control one's self, that creates disastrous consequences.[5]

The individuals who have committed mass murders might have been able to manage these feelings for years, or these feelings might have gone unrecognized by the individual. In some cases, a nonthreatening incident that normally would not be viewed as all that disruptive sends these individuals over the edge and triggers an angry, destructive, murderous response.

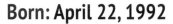

Born: April 22, 1992

Diagnosis: Anxiety, obsessive-
          compulsive disorder

Died: December 14, 2012

Adam Lanza's parents divorced when he was sixteen years old. Throughout his childhood and teenage years, Lanza exhibited a range of mental illness and special educational needs. At one point, his mother took him to Yale University's Child Study Center for an evaluation. The center made a series of recommendations, including medication, extensive special education services, and rigorous therapeutic support. His mother, Nancy, was Lanza's primary caregiver but never followed up on those recommendations. Lanza was also heavily engaged in an online community for mass-murder enthusiasts, where he fantasized about violence.

Lanza began his killing spree on the morning of December 14, 2012, when he shot his mother to death in her bed. He then drove to Sandy Hook Elementary School in Newtown, Connecticut, and forced his way into the building. Lanza stopped at one classroom and killed the teacher and all fourteen of her students. He then went to a second classroom where he killed the teacher and six of her students. Police arrived within one minute of the first 911 call. Witnesses reported hearing one final gunshot once authorities arrived on the scene. Adam Lanza killed himself with a gunshot to the head.

According to reports compiled after the Sandy Hook shootings, Lanza was "'completely untreated in the years before the shooting for psychiatric and physical ailments like anxiety and obsessive-compulsive disorder, and was also deprived of recommended services and drugs."[6] Many of Lanza's friends described him as deeply troubled and some family members say he suffered from Asperger's syndrome.[7] It was also determined by investigators that Lanza's mother sought to appease her son and instead of treating his disabilities, she accommodated him and ignored his behaviors.

Crime scene evidence shows firearms and ammunition found on or close to Adam Lanza's body at Sandy Hook Elementary School following the December 14, 2012, shooting rampage.

After the shooting, investigators found a spreadsheet where Lanza ranked mass murderers, a collection of articles, books and videos of mass murders, and an assembly of violent video games. A review of his computer found information suggesting that Lanza was fascinated with the Columbine High School massacre, the then-deadliest school shooting in history, which occurred on April 20, 1999.

In the weeks before the massacre, Lanza communicated with his mother only by e-mail, even though they lived in the same house together.

A study of the evidence following the Sandy Hook shooting found that Lanza was obsessed with mass murder, had

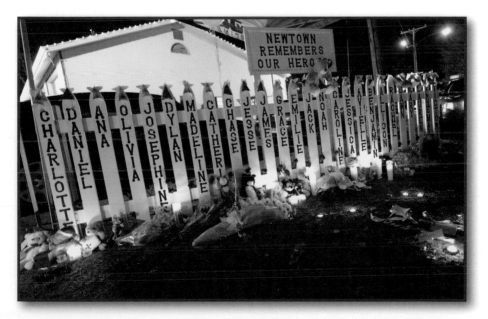

A picket fence with twenty-six posts represents each of the victims of the Sandy Hook Elementary School shooting in Newtown, Connecticut.

communicated via e-mail with mass murder enthusiasts he found online, and meticulously planned his attack.

Lanza's two violent acts—the murder of his mother and the massacre at Sandy Hook—were his only violent acts. There is no history of Lanza having had any previous violent tendencies. Evidence gathered during the investigation, plus extensive interviews with Lanza's father, brother, former teachers, and others, revealed that Lanza had significant mental health issues that went untreated and largely ignored. Police determined that Lanza might have been upset with his mother over the possibility of the two of them relocating to another town and this might have been a motivating factor. However, even after a lengthy investigation and consultation with those who knew Lanza well, no motive could be determined for why Lanza chose to carry out a shooting at an elementary school.

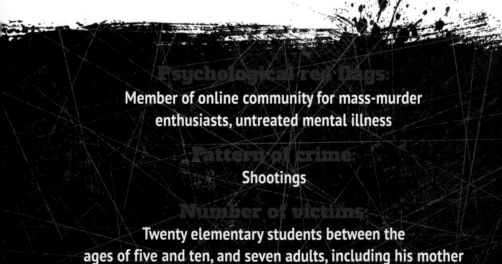

Psychological red flags:

Member of online community for mass-murder
enthusiasts, untreated mental illness

Pattern of crime:

Shootings

Number of victims:

Twenty elementary students between the
ages of five and ten, and seven adults, including his mother

Columbine High School Massacre

Eric Harris and Dylan Klebold

**Born: Eric Harris, April 9, 1981;
Dylan Klebold, September 11,
1981**

Occupations: High school students

**Diagnosis: Harris and Klebold
both suffered from psychopathy;
Klebold was diagnosed with
depression.**

Died: April 20, 1999

Eric Harris was born in Wichita, Kansas, but grew up on numerous military bases as a result of his family relocating often for his father's job as a pilot for the US Air Force. His mother was a stay-at-home mom who raised both Eric and his older brother. When his father retired from military service, the family settled in Littleton, Colorado.

Dylan Klebold was born and raised in Lakewood, Colorado, where his family was involved in a Lutheran church. He also had an older brother. Harris and Klebold became friends when Harris began attending Columbine High School.

Together, Harris and Klebold began getting into trouble. They made threats on a website toward another student and they broke into a van to steal computers. They were arrested for the break-in and robbery and sentenced to community service and a diversionary program. Unbeknownst to anyone, Harris and Klebold had begun planning an attack on their high school in the months before April 20, 1999, when they carried out what became the then-deadliest school shooting in US history. Initially, their plan was to place bombs in the cafeteria and gun down any survivors as they ran out of the school after the bombs went off. But when the bombs failed to detonate, they entered the school and began shooting students at random.

Columbine shooters Eric Harris (*left*) and Dylan Klebold appear on a surveillance tape in the cafeteria of Columbine High School.

Students run frantically from Columbine High School while protected by police.

Harris and Klebold killed themselves in the library of the school when law enforcement officers began to enter and take control of the building.

The Columbine High School massacre was organized and meticulously planned by Harris and Klebold. They arrived separately at the school. They placed duffle bags filled with bombs in the cafeteria before returning to their cars to arm themselves with shotguns and pipe bombs. They began shooting students outside the school first, before entering the school and heading to the cafeteria.

With the exception of their own brush with the law, Harris and Klebold offered few signs that anything was brewing before the

At the Columbine Memorial Park on April 20, 2009, in Littleton, Colorado, relatives and members of the community gathered to commemorate the ten-year anniversary of the Columbine High School shootings.

attack. In hindsight, Klebold's mother recalled her son being distant and quiet in the months before the attack.

After the shooting, investigators found the boys' diaries. Examination of the diaries indicated depression, psychopathic thoughts, and suicidal tendencies. It was also revealed that not only had they both kept diaries, they made a series of videos where both boys talked about their plans for the massacre. The boys also made videos that detailed a much more massive and deadly plan than what was ultimately carried out. Columbine was supposed to be a mass bombing, not a shooting. Their intention was for bombs to go off in the cafeteria during lunch, when the highest number of people would be in the room. As students fled, Harris and Klebold would gun them down outside. The final component of their plan was to take place when first responders and the media arrived. Car bombs were supposed to detonate to kill as many survivors and first responders as possible, all caught on live television by the media that arrived to cover the event. But Harris and Klebold wired the bombs poorly and they never detonated, so they entered the school to carry out an alternate plan.[8]

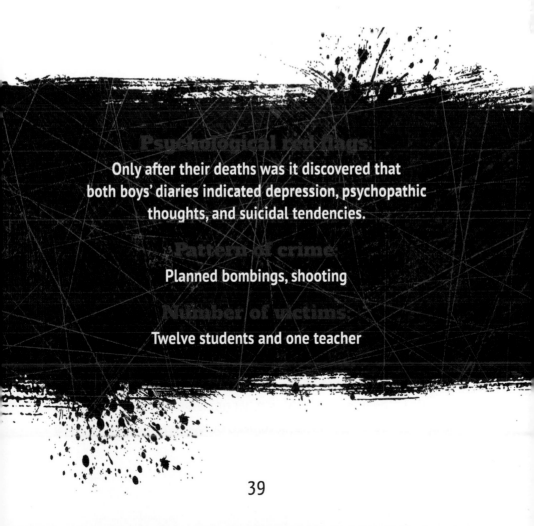

Psychological red flags:

Only after their deaths was it discovered that both boys' diaries indicated depression, psychopathic thoughts, and suicidal tendencies.

Pattern of crime:

Planned bombings, shooting

Number of victims:

Twelve students and one teacher

Assassination Attempt of Congresswoman Gabrielle Giffords

Jared Lee Loughner

Born: September 10, 1988

Diagnosis: Schizophrenia

Jared Lee Loughner attended Mountain View High School but dropped out before graduating. He earned his GED and began attending college, but friends and family reportedly told investigators that he experienced a radical personality transformation. Loughner had trouble keeping a job and was expelled from college. He experimented with drugs and was arrested for the possession of marijuana and drug paraphernalia. Loughner became paranoid and fearful that the government was out to get him. He began carrying a gun and got several tattoos of guns and bullets on his body.

Loughner had a dislike for Congresswoman Gabrielle Giffords. He felt women should not hold public office. His negative feelings for Giffords increased after he asked her a question at a constituent event that he felt she did not answer fully.

On January 8, 2011, Loughner walked up to Giffords while she was talking to two voters in a parking lot of a supermarket where she was holding an event. He shot her point blank in the head. Then he opened fire on the crowd; seventeen others were shot. Bystanders subdued Loughner until police arrived. Giffords sustained significant brain damage. Six of the victims died, including a nine-year-old girl.

To avoid the death penalty, Loughner pleaded guilty to nineteen federal charges and was sentenced to seven consecutive life sentences, plus 140 years.

Were there any signs of trouble before this act of terror? Loughner bought a gun months ahead of the attack, and the night before, he left a voicemail and social media post saying goodbye to friends. The morning of the attack, he bought ammunition at a local Walmart store before arriving at the scene.

Members of the sheriff's department guard the crime scene near the entrance of a Safeway store after Jared Loughner opened fire on a group of people, including US Representative Gabrielle Giffords.

Loughner's parents described his behavior in the months before the shooting as odd and concerning. His behavior grew delusional. His father took away his shotgun and often disabled his car at night so Loughner could not leave the house. Friends also witnessed a deterioration of his mental state. Loughner started drinking heavily in high school, had trouble with authorities, and had been expelled from college. His parents were urged to have him evaluated for mental illness. They never followed up.[9]

Loughner was diagnosed with schizophrenia after psychiatrists evaluated him in the months after the shooting.

Psychological red flags:

Delusional behavior, alcohol abuse, expulsion from college

Pattern of crime:

Shooting

Number of victims:

Six people were killed and eleven were wounded.

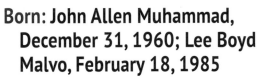

John Allen Muhammad and Lee Boyd Malvo

Born: John Allen Muhammad, December 31, 1960; Lee Boyd Malvo, February 18, 1985

Died: John Allen Muhammad, November 10, 2009, via lethal injection

John Allen Muhammad was born John Allen Williams in Baton Rouge, Louisiana. His mother died when he was three years old, and he was deserted by his father shortly after. His grandfather raised him. He joined the National Guard and served for seventeen years. He later joined the Nation of Islam, an Islamic religious movement that served to improve the mental, social, and spiritual lives of African Americans in the United States.

Muhammad befriended Lee Boyd Malvo's mother on the Caribbean twin-island nation of Antigua and Barbuda. They developed a close friendship, with Malvo's mother leaving him in Muhammad's care when she was deported.

Muhammad had several brushes with the law prior to his killing sprees, including restraining orders taken out against him by his two ex-wives. He also engaged in credit card fraud and possessed counterfeit immigration documents. Malvo, raised by a single mother who left him often in the care of others, was shuffled around during his childhood and established few ties with adults who could lead him in a positive direction. Seeking guidance and acceptance, Malvo, who was abused by his father, saw Muhammad as a savior who took him away from the difficult life he was living.

The terror began in the early morning hours of October 2, 2002. Malvo and Muhammad worked as a team as they carried out a series of attacks on random individuals along Interstate 95, referred to locally as the Beltway. One would select a victim while the other pulled the trigger. The first victim was James Martin, an analyst for the National Oceanic and Atmospheric Association, who they shot

During the murder trial for John Allen Muhammad, Lee Boyd Malvo is brought into court to be identified by a witness.

Sniper suspect John Allen Muhammad arrives in court. He was found guilty and sentenced to death by lethal injection.

and killed in the parking lot of a grocery store in Glenmont, Virginia. It continued on October 3, when four people were shot and killed over the span of two hours, and another two victims were killed later than night. More shootings occurred, on October 4, October 7, October 11, October 14, October 19, and October 22. In each attack, the pattern of attack was the same. Each victim was killed by a single bullet, all fired from a distance, while the victim was outside at a public location.

After the ninth killing, the pair sent a letter to local law enforcement asking for $10 million to end the killing spree. A phone call made by an unknown person directed police to a crime scene in Montgomery, Alabama. It was here where authorities identified Muhammad as a suspect from a fingerprint Muhammad left on a document at the scene. The fingerprint was a key piece of evidence that helped to break open the case for authorities and lead them to Malvo and Muhammad.

The Beltway sniper attacks paralyzed the people of Virginia and the District of Columbia area. People stayed inside, some schools were closed, and security at government buildings and tourist locations, such as the National Mall, was heightened. John Allen Muhammad and Lee Boyd Malvo were finally captured on October 24 when they were found sleeping in their car at a rest stop.

Malvo and Muhammad were tried separately for their crimes. Malvo testified against Muhammad and provided the court with a more detailed description of their original three-phase plan. In phase one they intended to kill six people a day for thirty days. This plan fell apart quickly after heavy traffic derailed their escape plans. Phase two involved killing a pregnant woman at random and a police officer. At the officer's funeral, Muhammad and Malvo intended to place bombs to kill a large number of officers. In phase three, the pair planned to extort millions of dollars from the US government before traveling to Canada to recruit orphaned boys. They planned to train and arm these children and send them out to commit shootings. But Muhammad and Malvo were captured before any additional phases of their plan could be put into motion.

Malvo is serving six consecutive life sentences without possibility of parole for his direct involvement in six of the fourteen murders the pair committed as part of both the Beltway attacks and murders committed in the months leading up to the Beltway killing spree. He is serving out his sentence at Red Onion State Prison in Virginia. He later told the *Washington Post*, in an interview ten years after the Beltway attacks, that he recalled being brainwashed and manipulated by Muhammad.[11]

Muhammad was sentenced to death and died on November 10, 2009, by lethal injection at the Sussex State Prison in Virginia.

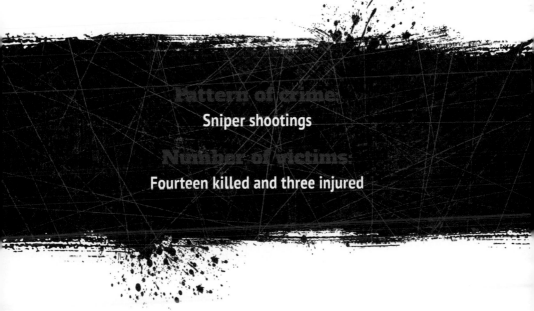

Pattern of crime

Sniper shootings

Number of victims

Fourteen killed and three injured

Chapter 3

Issue-Oriented Terrorism:
KILLING FOR A CAUSE

James Kopp tracked Dr. Barnett Slepian for almost a year. Weeks before he pulled the trigger and killed Slepian, Kopp traveled from his home in New Jersey to the Buffalo, New York, area to meticulously plan an attack on the doctor. Kopp buried a rifle in the woods behind Slepian's house, and on the evening of October 23, 1998, Kopp stood in the woods waiting for Slepian to return home. While Slepian stood in the kitchen with his family, Kopp shot and killed him through the kitchen window with a high-powered rifle. Slepian was an obstetrician who provided abortion services in the Buffalo area.[1] Kopp was an anti-abortion activist who believed that by killing Slepian, he was saving the lives of unborn children.

What Is Issue-Oriented Terrorism?

Slepian's murder is an example of issue-oriented terrorism. Those who carry out this type of terrorism are seeking to bring media attention to a particular issue or socially relevant topic. For those who kill for a cause, the killer might also see himself as providing a solution to a social problem. For example, Slepian's murder and other violent acts committed at abortion clinics are often viewed by the killer and his or her supporters as necessary to aid society and/or to protect innocent victims, such as unborn babies. These killers perceive their acts as noble and justifiable because they are

Two Erie County sheriff's officers lead James Kopp into court in Buffalo, NY, on August 19, 2002. Kopp was charged with killing Dr. Barnett Slepian, an obstetrician who performed abortions.

defending what they believe to be an innocent victim. Kopp, in an interview with the *Buffalo News*, told reporters that he needed to act when he did because there were several abortions scheduled for the next day. Killing Slepian was the best chance Kopp had to stop those abortions from happening.[2]

Ecoterrorism is a specific form of issue-oriented terrorism that focuses on taking action against the corporations or individuals that threaten animals or the environment. Ecoterrorism is more about causing damage to property, economically harming a corporation, and inflicting fear. Rarely do ecoterrorists kill in the name of their cause. These groups all have their own ideologies but all of them share three common characteristics: they have an uncompromising position in their beliefs, they are grassroots organizations, and they take direct action against their enemies.[3] Ecoterrorists are often radical environmentalists and fanatical animal-rights activists who seek extreme measures to get their messages across to the general public. These groups tend to use arson, bombings, and harassment as their key forms of terror.

Who Commits Issue-Oriented Terrorism and Why

People who commit acts of violence in the name of a cause often have a strong system of beliefs, such as a deeply religious devotion to their faith and its teachings, or are intensively devoted to the mission or vision of a particular cause. They also see violence as a way to prompt change. Many issue-oriented terrorists seek to harm or kill representatives of a particular government or group of people and target these people as their victims instead of the government or organization itself.

Born: April 23, 1968
Died: June 11, 2011

Timothy McVeigh was born in Lockport, New York, and was the second of three children. When he was ten, his parents divorced, and he moved with his father to Pendleton, New York. McVeigh joined the military and was deployed to the Persian Gulf for the first Gulf War in the early 1990s. He was awarded a Bronze Star for his service. He was later deployed to Operation Desert Storm. He was honorably discharged in 1991.

After his military service, McVeigh spoke critically of the US government. He talked about seeing the massive casualties of war and how he felt the US government had abused its power. He became increasingly pro gun and promoted pro-gun rights. He became a regular on the gun-show circuit, where gun dealers gather to exhibit new firearms and other weapons. At these shows, he began sharing his views on the evils of the government, which McVeigh began to believe was taking away people's rights.

McVeigh became influenced by two events involving federal agents. In the summer of 1992, Randy Weaver, a white separatist, was brought up on federal charges of selling illegal sawed-off shotguns. A standoff ensued at Weaver's cabin in Ruby Ridge, Idaho. In a shootout, federal agents killed Weaver's wife and son. In 1993,

Timothy McVeigh was given the death penalty for bombing a federal building in Oklahoma City, killing 168 people and injuring more than five hundred.

federal agents located the Waco, Texas, compound of the Branch Davidians, a religious cult led by David Koresh. Koresh had been in possession of illegal weapons. A fifty-one-day siege occurred between the US government and the Branch Davidians. On April 19, 1993, the standoff ended when the federal government attempted to forcibly remove the Branch Davidians. A fire erupted and eighty people, including Koresh and thirteen children, died in the blaze.

McVeigh began to view the US government as a bully who was trying to impede Americans' right to freedom and control gun rights.

He was angry with the federal government for what he deemed the misuse of its power in the events at Ruby Ridge and Waco. As a result, he began to meticulously plan the bombing of the Alfred P. Murrah Federal Building in Oklahoma City, Oklahoma.[4]

McVeigh and Terry Nichols, an accomplice in the bombing who McVeigh met in the military, chose the Alfred P. Murrah Federal Building for multiple reasons: its location provided good camera angles for media coverage and it was a federal building, which meant it housed offices of federal law enforcement agencies, including the Drug Enforcement Administration and the Bureau of Alcohol, Tobacco, and Firearms.

McVeigh and Nichols armed a rental van with explosives and parked it in front of the building just as business hours were beginning for the day. They chose the day, April 19, 1995, because it was the two-year anniversary of the Waco siege. The explosion destroyed more than a third of the building and damaged several other buildings close by. The blast killed 168 people, including nineteen children who were attending an on site day-care center, and injured more than five hundred.

McVeigh was arrested shortly after the bombing, when he was pulled over for driving without a license plate and for being in possession of illegal firearms. Three days later, he was officially identified as the bomber. McVeigh stood trial and was found guilty of all eleven federal counts, including conspiracy to use a weapon of mass destruction, use of a weapon of mass destruction, destruction by explosives, and eight counts of first-degree murder of federal law enforcement officers. A jury recommended the death penalty at his sentencing, and McVeigh was executed on June 11, 2011, by lethal injection.

The Alfred P. Murrah Federal Building in Oklahoma City was nearly destroyed by a fuel-and-fertilizer truck bomb that was detonated in front of the building.

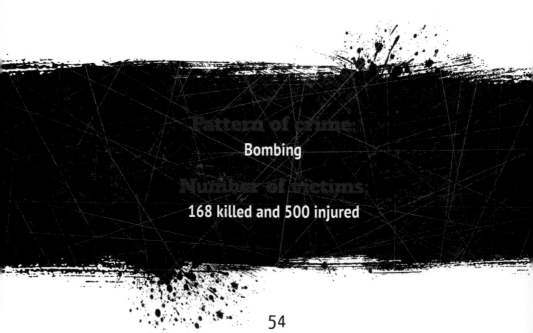

Pattern of crime:

Bombing

Number of victims:

168 killed and 500 injured

John C. Salvi

Born: March 2, 1972
Diagnosis: **Schizophrenia**
Died: November 29, 1996

John Salvi was born in Salem, Massachusetts. He was an only child. His father was a dental technician, and his mother was a choir director and piano teacher. His parents were very involved in their Catholic church while Salvi was growing up. He attended Catholic school until his father moved the family to Florida.

While in Florida, Salvi began getting into trouble. He was involved in several car accidents and was a suspect in numerous fires, including one that destroyed his father's storage space business. His father refused to press charges or to cooperate with authorities to pursue an investigation.

Salvi began to believe that the Freemasons, the world's oldest and largest fraternity, along with the Mafia and the Ku Klux Klan, were conspiring to persecute Catholics. He also began to support anti-abortion efforts and he became sympathetic to anti-abortion organizations that promoted violence against abortion clinics and abortion service providers. Salvi soon became involved in the Army of God, an extremist-Christian terrorist organization that encourages violence as a way to prevent abortions. The group has been tied to numerous violent acts against abortion clinics and providers since

John C. Salvi, right, speaks with his lawyer. Salvi killed two people and injured five in shootings at abortion clinics.

the early 1980s. Salvi joined more than 300 anti-abortion demonstrators in the spring of 1994. They protested outside of a Planned Parenthood clinic in Brookline, Massachusetts.

John Salvi also showed some signs of emotional disturbance in the days leading up to the abortion clinic shootings. Salvi met with a Catholic priest and demanded that he be given permission to distribute photographs of aborted fetuses. Salvi felt that the Catholic Church was not doing enough to stop abortions or abortion providers. Frustrated by what he perceived to be a lack of response from the Catholic Church, Salvi decided to take matters into his own hands. Salvi carefully choose two locations for the shootings. In addition, he purchased a .22 caliber hunting rifle at a gun store in the weeks leading up to his terror attacks at the clinics.

On December 30, 1994, Salvi walked into that same Brookline Planned Parenthood clinic where he'd previously protested and asked the receptionist if he was in an abortion-services clinic. When she confirmed, Salvi shot her to death. He then turned and sprayed gunfire into the lobby. He fled the building, got into his truck and drove two miles down Beacon Street to Preterm Health Services. Again, he confirmed that abortions were among the clinic's services before he opened fire and killed the receptionist. He also shot into the lobby of the clinic, which was full of people. An on-duty security guard returned fire and Salvi fled, but not before he dropped a bag. In it was ammunition, another gun, and a receipt from a gun store for the rifle he used in the killings.[5]

Law enforcement was able to identify Salvi from the receipt, and a manhunt ensued. The next day, Salvi was captured when he entered the lobby of another women's clinic in Norfolk, Virginia. There, he opened fire, but no one in that shooting was injured. Police responding to the Norfolk shooting detained Salvi, and shortly afterwards, from the gun-store receipt, descriptions provided by gun-store employees, and witnesses at both the Brookline shootings, law enforcement was able to positively identify Salvi as the suspect in the Brookline shootings.

Salvi was mentally evaluated after the Planned Parenthood attack and was diagnosed by a psychiatrist as suffering from schizophrenia. He was charged with two counts of first-degree murder and five counts of armed assault with intent to murder for the shootings in Brookline. On March 19, 1996, Salvi was convicted of all seven counts. He was sentenced to two consecutive life-sentence terms plus eighteen to twenty years for assault convictions. On November 29, 1996, Salvi was found dead in his prison cell with a plastic garbage bag over his head. His death was ruled a suicide.[6]

Pattern of crime:

Shootings

Number of victims:

Two killed, five injured

Arson at Vail Resorts in Vail, Colorado

Earth Liberation Front

Earth Liberation Front

Date of incident: October 19, 1998

The Earth Liberation Front's mission is to cause as much economic damage as possible to the people and corporations that profit from the destruction of the environment and the exploitation of its natural resources. ELF, whose members call themselves "Elves," has set fire to or bombed a wide range of buildings in an effort to cause extensive property damage and economic pain for the companies or people responsible for the construction of these projects.

One such example of ELF's activities occurred on October 19, 1998, when ELF supporters set fire to three buildings and four chairlifts at Vail Resorts, one of the largest ski resorts in Vail, Colorado. In an e-mail sent to media, ELF stated, "Vail, Inc. is already the largest ski operation in North America and now wants to expand even further. The twelve miles of roads and 885 acres of clearcuts will ruin the last, best lynx habitat in the state. Putting profits ahead of Colorado's wildlife will not be tolerated."[7]

ELF set fire to the resort in reaction to the planned expansion of the resort into an area that was a potential habitat for the reintroduction of the Canadian lynx, an endangered species of wildcat that conservationists had been trying to restore to North America.

Arson investigators search for clues at the remnants of the dining facility on the top of Vail Resorts.

The resort had begun clearing land the previous week to begin an eight-hundred-acre expansion project that would include numerous new ski trails.

Prior to the arson at Vail Resorts, ELF had taken responsibility for five other arsons at federal buildings in Oregon and Washington State, and at several locations in the west.

ELF's pattern of attack has been the systematic use of bombings and arson. Chelsea Dawn Gerlach and Stanislas Gregory Meyerhoff, members of ELF, both plead guilty to the Vail Resorts arson. The pair was found to be responsible for arsons committed between

1996 and 2001 in Oregon, Colorado, and Washington State that caused more than $20 million in damage to an electrical transmission tower, a timber research center, and a police station.[8] The arson at Vail Resorts destroyed a ski patrol headquarters building, a skier shelter, a mountaintop restaurant, and several chairlifts. Gerlach was sentenced to nine years in prison. Meyerhoff was sentenced to thirteen years in prison.

Pattern of crime:

Bombings and arson

Number of victims:

No one was killed or injured in these events.

Chapter 4

Political Terrorism:

INFLUENCING CHANGE THROUGH VIOLENCE

The Ku Klux Klan rose to power in the South in the late 1870s at the end of the American Civil War, when the Union government of the North began to enact and enforce laws designed to end the segregation of blacks. The group began its systemic intimidation of blacks when the Fifteenth Amendment gave blacks the right to vote. They used arson, rape, harassment, and lynching to intimidate blacks and anyone sympathetic to their cause. The group has had periods of inaction, but became active when political measures were being debated to provide equal rights to blacks, such as during the civil rights movement. The modern Klan has expanded its targets to include other factions of society, including the LGBT community, Muslims, Jews, and immigrants.

POLITICAL TERRORISM: INFLUENCING CHANGE THROUGH VIOLENCE

For centuries, the Klan has sought to eradicate or eliminate blacks through an ideology of purification, or the idea that only one group (whites) is worthy of prospering and leading society. Through violence and murder, they have sought out, tortured, and killed black men and women in public displays of their power.

What Is Political Terrorism?

The Klan is among the oldest and most infamous of hate groups, whose actions are solely designed to terrorize and intimidate. They are political terrorists.

Political terrorists use violence to coerce or intimidate a government or civilian population to further the terrorists' political or social objectives. It also involves an all-encompassing moral philosophy that is used to justify acts of violence to produce what the terrorist believes to be an improved overall social state.

Political and religious terrorism can sometimes overlap, as was seen in the September 11 terrorist attacks and the Oklahoma City bombing, with attacks having signs of both. But, upon closer review, political terrorism is rooted more in attacks that seek to produce social change rather than attacks that serve as punishment. While the September 11 terrorist attacks had a political undertone, the attacks were primarily a function of religious extremism. The same can be said of the Oklahoma City bombing, an event that was fundamentally religious versus political in nature, even though the target of the bombing was a federal building housing government offices and personnel.

Right-wing terrorism aims to combat liberal governments and to preserve traditional social orders. A liberal government or ideology is one that believes in equality for all people, regardless of their gender, sexual orientation, religion, ethnicity, or nationality. Traditional social orders refer to a set of social structures, customs, values, and practices all shared by a common group of people. The Ku Klux Klan, for example, seeks to keep or restore the supremacy of white people and isolate, intimidate, and disillusion any group different from them.

In other words, right-wing terrorism views any sort of progress in the inclusion or acceptance of minority groups in the United States as a threat. Right-wing terrorists are often members of militias or white-supremacy groups, such as the Ku Klux Klan, looking to banish any and all minority groups, including traditional minority groups, such as Jews, Catholics, and blacks, as well as emerging and growing minority groups, such as Muslims, gays, immigrants, and members of emerging religions. Hate crimes against minorities are right-wing terrorist acts.

What Causes People to Adopt a Political Cause as a Motivation for Terrorist Activity?

Political terrorists want to create a long-term atmosphere of fear and intimidation in society to produce societal change. The Ku Klux Klan, for example, has been around for more than a century, and has fought against political decisions, such as giving black Americans the right to vote and the passing of civil rights legislation.

For groups professing political or social motivations, their targets are usually symbolic, such as government offices, churches, banks, or multinational corporations. They also use race and differences in political opinions as a motivation to commit terrorist acts.

The Ku Klux Klan terrorists have used violence and murder against black men and women in public displays of their power.

Dylann Roof

Born: April 3, 1994

Dylann Roof was born in Columbia, South Carolina. His father was a carpenter and his mother was a bartender. His parents' marriage was a troubled one, and the couple broke up and got back together numerous times until they finally divorced when Roof was a toddler. His father remarried, but that marriage failed ten years later.

Roof bounced around to a number of schools. He exhibited signs of obsessive-compulsive disorder. He quit school in 2010, when he was in ninth grade. In 2015, he was arrested twice. The first arrest came after he went to the Columbia Centre, a local mall, and began asking strange and unsettling questions to salespeople. While being questioned by police, law enforcement found he was carrying a bottle of Suboxone, a narcotic. He was arrested for drug possession and banned from the Columbia Centre. He was arrested a month later, when he violated the mall's ban.

A week later, on June 17, 2015, Roof allegedly entered the Emanuel African Methodist Episcopal (AME) Church, a historical church that had been founded by worshippers who were fleeing the racism of the South in the 1700s. The church, which has a storied history, was home to freed blacks and slaves alike since its founding in 1791, and was a constant presence in the lives of blacks living in

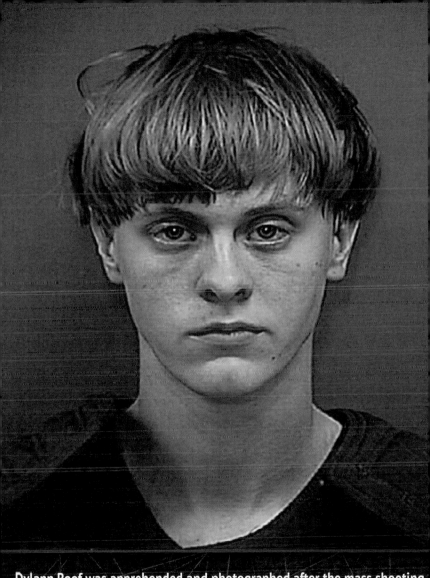

Dylann Roof was apprehended and photographed after the mass shooting at the Emanuel African Methodist Episcopal Church in Charleston, South Carolina. He was suspected of killing nine people during a prayer meeting

Charleston. When laws were in place in the 1800s that prohibited blacks from gathering without white supervision, the congregation worshipped in secret. Over the course of its nearly two hundred thrity year history, the church has been burned down and rebuilt, has survived earthquakes, and was an influential stop for civil rights leaders.[1] It has served as a symbol of black freedom. Roof later told investigators he purposefully choose the church for its ties to the black community and for its historical significance.

When Roof arrived at the Emanuel AME Church, he joined a Bible study group already in progress. He stayed for nearly an hour before he pulled out a gun and opened fire. He killed nine parishioners,

Congregants hold up photographs of the nine victims killed at the Emanuel AME Church in Charleston during a prayer vigil at the Metropolitan AME Church on June 19, 2015, in Washington, DC.

including the church's pastor, Clementa Pinckney. Pinckney was also a South Carolina state senator. All of Roof's victims were black.

During the shooting, Roof intentionally spared the lives of three people so that survivors could tell others what had happened inside the church. Three people survived the attack and later told police that Roof had told them during the shooting that "you rape our women and you're taking over our country. You have to go." According to one survivor, Roof reloaded his gun five times.

Roof began making various racist comments in the months leading up to the shooting. According to neighbors, Roof told them he was going to kill black people, even mentioning the College of Charleston as a possible target.[2] His neighbors did not take his claims seriously.

Roof fled after the shooting, but was captured the next day by law enforcement during a traffic stop. He was charged with nine counts of murder and one count of possession of a firearm during the commission of a violent crime. As of the publication date of this title, Roof has pled not guilty to the charges and is awaiting trial.

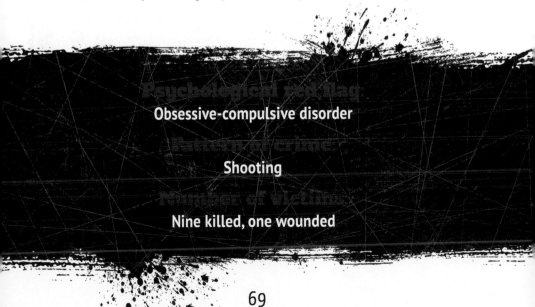

Psychological red flag:
Obsessive-compulsive disorder

Pattern of crime:
Shooting

Number of victims:
Nine killed, one wounded

Wade Michael Page

Born: November 11, 1971

Died: August 5, 2012

Wade Michael Page was an Army veteran who was also a musician. He played in numerous bands, including Blue Eyed Devils and another called Definite Hate. The bands wrote and performed songs with lyrics about killing minority groups. The bands were part of the "white power" music scene, which is categorized by hateful lyrics and performances in which Neo-Nazi symbolism is heavily used.

Page spent his childhood in Colorado, where his family spent weekends camping. He lost his mother when he was in his early teens and he struggled to cope with her death.

After high school, Page joined the US Army and was stationed at military installations around the United States. He was never deployed overseas. He became an accomplished parachutist and earned awards. In 1995, Page was stationed at Fort Bragg, Fayetteville, North Carolina. Fort Bragg, at the time, had a strong and powerful subculture of white supremacy. Many soldiers recruited members for the National Alliance, which was one of the nation's best organized and most well-financed Neo-Nazi organizations. Many soldiers openly flew the Nazi flag and played music encouraging the killing of minorities. It is believed that Page first began his interest in Neo-Nazism while stationed at the army base.

Wade Michael Page fired upon people at a service at the Sikh Temple of Wisconsin. The United States Army veteran was killed in a shootout with police.

Page was discharged from the Army after getting drunk on duty and for being absent without leave, which means he did not have the military's permission to be away from his base.[3] Later, he joined several different bands, all of which described themselves as racist skinhead bands on their social-media profiles. These bands' violent songs promoted hate and Neo-Nazi idealism, and were laced with lyrics about murdering Jews, black people, gays, and other people Page and his band mates deemed as enemies. The Southern Poverty Law Center began tracking Page for his involvement in rock bands that promoted hateful, violent messages. The SPLC is a legal advocacy group that specialized in civil rights. The group routinely monitors hate groups and extremists. Page came to the attention of the SPLC when he joined racist white-supremacy bands and when he tried to purchase goods from the National Alliance.[4]

On August 5, 2012, at around 10:30 a.m., Page entered the Sikh Temple of Wisconsin in Oak Creek. At the time, the church was filled with people attending worship services as well as preparing lunch for parishioners. Page opened fire inside the temple. As he exited, he encountered law enforcement officers that were responding to 911 calls about the shooting. Page engaged in a shootout with officers. Page was shot in the stomach and collapsed. Before he could be detained and his weapon secured, Page shot himself in the head. Killed in the attack were the president of the temple, three priests, and two parishioners. A police officer was shot outside the temple, but survived.

Page purchased the handgun used in the shootings at a gun shop in West Allis, Wisconsin, on July 28, 2012. According to reports, he passed all of the required background checks. He paid cash for a semi-automatic pistol and three nineteen-round magazines.

Family and friends gather at Oak Creek High School to mourn the loss of six members of the Sikh Temple of Wisconsin.

Pattern of crime:

Shooting

Number of victims:

Six killed, one injured

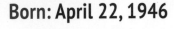

Born: April 22, 1946

Occupation: Microbiologist; senior biodefense researcher at the United States Army Medical Research Institute of Infectious Diseases

Diagnosis: Depression

Died: July 29, 2008

Bruce Edwards Ivins was born in Lebanon, Ohio. His father was a pharmacist who owned a drug store and his mother was a homemaker. He was the youngest of three boys. At an early age, Ivins excelled in science. He attended the University of Cincinnati, where he earned a bachelor's degree, a master's degree, and a doctorate—all in microbiology. He was well respected in his field and published more than forty-four research papers.

Ivins worked for more than eighteen years at the United States Army Medical Research Institute of Infectious Diseases. This government agency conducts scientific research to produce antidotes against biological weapons. Biological warfare is the use of bacteria and viruses to harm or kill people in an act of war. Ivins was a co-inventor on two US patents for anthrax vaccines. Anthrax is a disease caused by a specific bacterium and most often leads to death for those who are exposed to it.[5]

POLITICAL TERRORISM: INFLUENCING CHANGE THROUGH VIOLENCE

In 2001, a few weeks after the 9/11 terrorist attacks, anonymous letters laced with anthrax began arriving at the offices of media companies and members of the US Senate.[6] The letters contained messages of anti-American sentiment and led investigators to initially believe that they might have been sent by al-Qaeda, which had taken responsibility for the 9/11 terrorist attacks. The nation, already in a heightened state of fear and anxiety, was now facing a new and undetectable threat: biological warfare.

Over the course of three months, from September through November of 2001, numerous letters laced with anthrax were mailed to a number of media outlets, including ABC News, CBS News, NBC News, and the *New York Post*, as well as to two prominent US senators, Senate Majority Leader Tom Daschle and Senator Patrick Leahy. It is believed by investigators that Ivins's motive was to terrorize the nation in an effort to save an anthrax vaccine program that he had helped to create but that the government deemed a failure.

At first, Ivins was part of the biological team assessing the strain of anthrax used in the letters, but he soon became a suspect in the events. He not only had access to the specific strain used in the letters, but there were work hours during the time period when the letters were mailed that were unaccounted for by Ivins.

While there is little evidence of mental illness during the period when anthrax-laced letters were mailed, Ivins began to have problems during the federal government's investigation of him as a suspect in the crime. He made threats against coworkers at his lab, and a therapist treating Ivins requested an order of protection against him for making homicidal threats toward her.

Investigators believe that Ivins created the anthrax spores used in the attack. He wrote misleading letters implicating a terrorist

TOM BROKAW
NBC TV
30 ROCKEFELLER PLAZA
NEW YORK NY 10112

101 ...002

Letter to Tom Brokaw

4TH GRADE
GREENDALE SCHOOL
FRANKLIN PARK NJ 08852

SENATOR DASCHLE
509 HART SENATE OFFICE
BUILDING
WASHINGTON D.C. 2051...

20510/4103

Letter to Senator Daschle

Bruce Ivins sent letters containing anthrax bacteria to NBC in New York and to the Washington, DC, office of US senator Tom Daschle. Both letters were postmarked in Trenton, New Jersey, and the handwriting on the envelopes matched.

organization, and drove to New Jersey to mail the letters in an attempt to mislead the investigation.

Lab reports showed that Ivins logged hours of evening time in his lab just before the letters were mailed. Ivins also had several unexplained absences when investigators believe Ivins drove to New Jersey to mail the letters. Quickly, investigators determined that the letters were mailed from within the United States and were not connected to a foreign terrorist group.

Over the course of three months, five people died from anthrax exposure, including two postal workers who handled the contaminated letters. Another seventeen were infected by the bacterium.

The investigation into the case took years. In 2008, Bruce Ivins lost his security clearance at work due to changes in his behavior. Later that year, he lost access to restricted areas of his lab. He soon entered a psychiatric hospital, where he made statements to other people about the anthrax letters and the resulting deaths. Shortly after entering the hospital, the FBI informed Ivins that they were actively investigating him and that they were on the verge of filing criminal charges against him in this case.

In July 27, 2008, Ivins was found unconscious in his home. He died two days later from an overdose of Tylenol PM, a painkiller containing a sleeping aid.

Ivins misled investigators by lying about his ability to create the specific anthrax spores used in the letters in the lab. In a Department of Justice summary of the case against Ivins, it was determined that he held a grudge against senators Daschle and Leahy, who were both pro-choice in their stance on abortion. In 2010, a report issued by the FBI, Department of Justice, and the US Postal Inspection

Service formally concluded their lengthy investigations of the anthrax mailings. The report announced that the three agencies determined that Ivins mailed the anthrax letters.[7]

Pattern of crime:

Anthrax contamination

Number of victims:

Five killed; seventeen infected

Chapter 5

Narcotics-Based Terrorism:

KILLING FOR CONTROL OF THE DRUG MARKET

The US Southern Command headquarters, located just outside of Miami, Florida, is tasked with countering the activities of some of the most powerful and violent criminal drug cartels and terrorist groups in the world. The Command monitors and detects drug-trafficking activities in South America, Central America, and the Caribbean—all of which are home to the most powerful and influential drug cartels and terrorist organizations that operate the international drug trade. The Command supports US law enforcement operations in this region of the world. They also serve as an operational and analytical hub for America's efforts to fight against drug and terrorism activities in Latin America.[1] Through their analysis of illegal activities, they are the organization that connects the dots. The organization is able to tie unrelated activity—from the movements of drug cartel leaders, the rise in drug epidemics in certain countries, and seemingly unexplained murders—to drugs and terrorism.

Southern Command knew that when Joaquín Archivaldo "El Chapo" Guzmán Loera, the leader of the Sinaloa cartel, escaped from a Mexican super-maximum-security prison in 2015, it wasn't luck. His escape had more to do with the strength and reach of the Sinaloa cartel and other major Mexican drug-trafficking organizations.

The US Southern Command headquarters is located near Miami, Florida. It fights against the activities of some of the most powerful and violent criminal drug cartels and terrorist groups in the world.

Joaquín "El Chapo" Guzmán is taken into custody in 2014. The world's most-wanted drug boss escaped after this capture but was recaptured in January 2016.

What Is Narcotics-Based Terrorism?

Narcotics-based terrorism, also called narcoterrorism, is terrorism that is associated with the illegal movement and sale of drugs. The violence that results is due in large part to the attempts of drug cartels that traffic drugs to influence the policies of a government or a society through violence and intimidation. They also rely on violence as a method of control. The threat of violence against a government official, or his or her family members, can keep that official from conducting investigations and hinder the enforcement of anti-drug laws.

Who Commits Narcoterrorism and Why?

Drug-related terrorism is often designed to make the sale of drugs easier or to intimidate governments and their officials. Pablo Escobar, a notorious Colombian drug lord, ordered the assassinations of Colombian politicians during the height of his power in the late 1980s. He did this to intimidate the Colombian government and its various political leaders so they would leave him and his cartel alone and allow them to conduct their drug-trafficking business without interference.

The Connection Between Drugs and Terrorism

Narcoterrorism also refers to the joint efforts between drug cartels and established terrorist groups who have partnered together to make their individual efforts stronger, or to mislead authorities in their investigations. According to statistics by the US Drug Enforcement Agency, nearly 40 percent of the terrorist groups designated by the US State Department are now involved in drug trafficking.[2]

A report by the United Nations Office on Drugs and Crime states that "drug trafficking has provided funding for insurgency and those who use terrorist violence in various regions throughout the world, including in transit regions. In some cases, drugs have even been the currency used in the commission of terrorist attacks, as was the case in the Madrid bombings."[3] At a worldwide conference on drugs and terrorism, titled "The Role of Drug Trafficking in Promoting and Financing Today's Global Terrorism," members of counterterrorism agencies from the United States, Colombia, Turkey, and officials from the United Nations Office on Drugs and Crime all agreed that the cooperation between terrorist groups and drug cartels is a large, international problem that needs attention.

Pablo Escobar

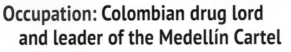

> **Occupation: Colombian drug lord
> and leader of the Medellín Cartel**
> **Born: December 1, 1949**
> **Died: December 2, 1993**

Pablo Escobar was born on December 1, 1949, in Rionegro, Colombia. His father worked as a peasant farmer while his mother was a schoolteacher. From an early age, Escobar wanted to become president of Colombia. But he soon began a life of crime. He started as a petty street thief, moved onto stealing cars, and then became involved in the smuggling business. He gained early success as a key player in Colombia's smuggling of cigarettes. He later started smuggling drugs. He was arrested for possession of cocaine. He attempted to bribe the judges who were building the case against him. When that didn't work, he had the two police officers who arrested him killed. This was the beginning of Escobar's terror campaigns to control the Colombian government.

As demand for drugs increased, especially in the United States, Escobar organized more smuggling operations, mapped out smuggling routes, and developed delivery networks throughout South America. Escobar's Medellín cartel was formed, and at the height of its influence, the cartel was shipping as much as eleven tons of drugs in airliners around the world. It is estimated that Escobar controlled

Pablo Escobar, head of the Medellín cartel, was photographed in Colombia in February 1988.

80 percent of the global cocaine market. He became known world-wide as his cartel grew in power and dominance.

Part of the reason the Medellín cartel became so powerful was Escobar's violence toward law enforcement. He had one policy, called "Plato o plomo," which is Spanish for "silver or lead." He offered government officials, politicians, and others who stood in his way one of two choices: silver, meaning they could accept a monetary bribe, or lead, meaning they could be shot to death with bullets. Escobar bribed hundreds of government officials, judges, politicians, police chiefs, and others during his life as a cartel leader. He also ordered the murders of countless others, including Colombian presidential candidate Luis Carlos Galán.

It is also alleged that Escobar oversaw the bombing of Avianca Flight 203, a passenger plane traveling from Bogota to Cali, Colombia. Five minutes into the flight, a bomb detonated and the plane was destroyed, killing all 107 passengers and crew on board. Escobar ordered the bombing because he wanted to kill César Gaviria Trujillo, a Colombian presidential candidate. Gaviria was not on board.

Escobar also rewarded his hit men for killing police officers by giving them large amounts of cash. As a result, more than six hundred Colombian police officers died. Escobar's campaign of terror also included journalists who did not write favorably about him or asked too many intrusive questions.

One of the reasons that Escobar was able to succeed in his campaign of terror was that he was well-protected—by his own cartel associates, by bodyguards who personally protected him, and by the residents of Medellín. Escobar was very philanthropic toward the people in his city. He built sports complexes, hospitals, schools, and churches; brought electricity to the more isolated areas of the town; and funded the construction of homes for the poor. The people of Medellín considered him their hero, and they repaid him by serving as lookouts for law enforcement entering town. They also hid information from the authorities and lied about Escobar's location.[4]

After the assassination of Galan, Cesar Gaviria, who was elected president of Colombia, began to take power away from Escobar as he cracked down on drug trafficking and the activities of the Medellín cartel. Gaviria offered Escobar a lighter sentence if he ceased all drug activity and gave himself up. Escobar surrendered and was sentenced to prison. But when authorities found he was still running his cartel from behind bars, they tried to move him to another prison, and Escobar escaped.

The United States partnered with the Colombian government, and many of Escobar's rival cartels began to join forces to fund Escobar. A manhunt ensued for Escobar. His reign as the world's most famous drug king came to an end on December 2, 1993, when Colombian National Police located him in the city of Medellín. They tried to capture him, but Escobar fled when authorities closed in on him. He was shot when he tried to run.

Escobar was consistent and unwavering, which meant government officials and law enforcement agencies took him seriously. He was able to gain a lot of power this way. Escobar's campaign of terror lasted more than forty years, and over that time members of his cartel used assassinations, car bombings, shootings, and kidnappings as their means of violence.

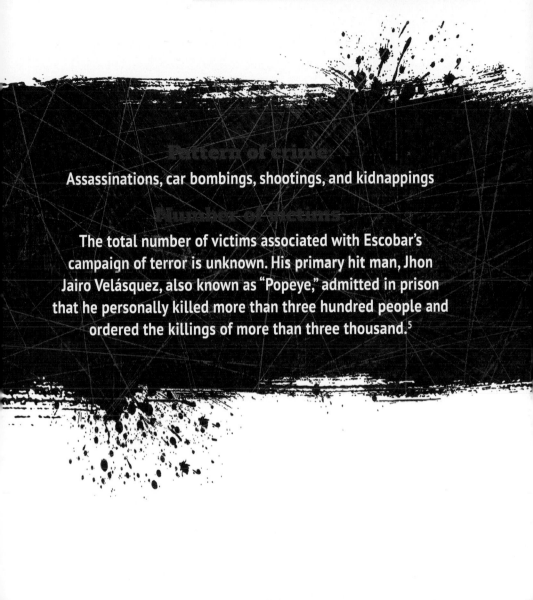

Pattern of crime

Assassinations, car bombings, shootings, and kidnappings

Number of victims

The total number of victims associated with Escobar's campaign of terror is unknown. His primary hit man, Jhon Jairo Velásquez, also known as "Popeye," admitted in prison that he personally killed more than three hundred people and ordered the killings of more than three thousand.[5]

Madrid Train Bombings

Islamic militants; local coordinator was Serhane ben Abdelmajid Fakhet

On March 11, 2004, as morning commuters piled into train cars on the Cercanías, the commuter train system in Madrid, Spain, ten coordinated bombings occurred on four separate trains over the course of thirteen minutes. All four trains were traveling on the same line and in the same direction.

The bombs were hidden in backpacks and other small bags that had been placed on the trains.[6] Shortly after the blast, al-Qaeda claimed responsibility. But investigators found that a terror cell responsible for the bombings funded the attack with illegal drugs. The bombers apparently obtained the dynamite from petty criminals in a coal-mining region of northern Spain who accepted drugs as payment.[7] The bombers traded drugs for more than 440 pounds of dynamite. The bombers also used proceeds from drug sales to rent an apartment, buy a car, and purchase cell phones and other materials used to detonate the bombs. The man in charge of the group's finances was Jamal Ahmidan, a thirty-three-year-old Moroccan immigrant with an extensive criminal record for drug trafficking. Ahmidan, along with the mastermind of the bombing, Serhane ben Abdelmajid Fakhet, and five other suspects, blew themselves up as police got closer to connecting them to the attack and began to move in to capture the men.

Seven months after the bombings, several wire-tapped conversations of one of the alleged organizers of the terrorist attack were reported to the public and revealed a possible motive. The conversation suggests the bombings were carefully timed to take place three days before a Spanish national election in hopes of influencing Spanish voters to reject a government that sent troops

The Madrid train attack was the result of bombs hidden on four trains by terrorists.

to Iraq. Spain served as a key ally to the United States in the war on Iraq. It is suspected that the attacks were planned because of Spain's support of the United States and to influence the outcome of the election.

The attacks seemed to accomplish their goal. The Populist Party, the ruling party in control of the Spanish government when the bombs went off, had a lead in the polls going into the election. Fighting terrorism was a primary goal of Prime Minister José María Alfredo Aznar. However, more than 90 percent of Spaniards opposed Aznar's support of the United States in the war against Iraq. The bombings renewed voters' interest in each candidate's position on the war in the final hours of the election. Aznar's Populist Party lost on election day, which occurred three days after the bombings. The Socialist Party, which won the election, had pledged during their campaign to withdraw thirteen hundred Spanish troops from Iraq if they won the election.

Ultimately, twenty-one people were found guilty in a Spanish court for their participation in the Madrid train bombings, though more are suspected of being involved. Those suspects have either fled the country before being captured or killed themselves to avoid being arrested.

Pattern of crime

Bombing

Number of victims

199 killed; more than 1,450 injured

Monterrey Casino Attack of 2011

Los Zetas cartel

Monterrey, which is located about 140 miles south of the Texas border, is a relatively wealthy Mexican city. Home to more than four million people, Monterrey is also the headquarters of some major Mexican companies, such as Cemex and Grupo Bimbo, as well as manufacturing facilities operated by Mercedes, BMW, Samsung, Boeing, and General Electric.[8] From 2008 to 2011, the city found itself at the center of a series of drug-related terrorist events. As conflicts between the major Mexican drug cartels grew, Monterrey experienced an influx of violence as cartels openly fought one another in the streets. The city's close proximity to the American border is key for drug smugglers. Violence in the city had been increasing as drug cartels battled for control of the area, which would give them control of access points to the United States. As shootouts, robberies, and extortion increased, the wave of violence tarnished the city's reputation as one of the best Latin American cities for investment and entrepreneurship. Traditionally, cartels limited their violence to gangsters, cartel members, and law enforcement. But the fighting between the cartels took a drastically different turn on August 25, 2011, when armed gunmen entered Casino Royale.

While customers gambled and played games of chance, four vehicles pulled up outside. Several armed gunmen carrying containers of gasoline entered the building. While they ordered people to get out, panic ensued with people running from the scene, hiding in bathrooms, and trying to escape in blocked stairwells. The gunman set fire to the casino's gambling machines and card tables. Smoke and flames filled the casino. The building burst into flames and many of the victims were trapped. By the time rescue crews could enter the building, fifty-two people had died and dozens were hospitalized with injuries and burns.[9]

A week later, five suspects were arrested in connection with the casino arson, all of them members of the Los Zetas drug cartel.[10] The cartel is suspected of ordering the attack on the casino, whose owners were being extorted by the cartel and reportedly had failed to pay protection money to Los Zetas. According to statements made by the suspects, the arson was intended as punishment to the casino owners and not meant as a civilian attack. They said their cartel bosses were angry that so many people had died in the fire.

Violence between Mexican drug cartels had been escalating for years. And the killing of civilians had become more and more common. In September 2008, cartel members threw two grenades into a crowd celebrating Mexico's Independence Day, killing eight people. In July 2010, another cartel set off a car bomb that killed police and civilians.

Los Zetas was part of the Gulf cartel but broke away and established itself as a separate criminal organization. In an attempt to gain new territory in Mexico, Los Zetas began a string of violent terrorist acts across Mexico, including the massacres of seventy-two migrants working at a ranch in the city of San Fernando. Los Zetas

Five members of the Los Zetas drug cartel participated in the attack of the Casino Royale.

is considered the most technologically advanced and sophisticated of the Mexican drug cartels. They are also the largest drug cartel in terms of territory. The cartel is funded through drug trafficking but also by extortion and protection fees paid to them by those they are extorting or by individuals seeking protection from rival cartels.

Five of the twelve gunman were arrested a week after the fire. They were detained after their arrests and charged with homicide and organized crime activity. They were later sentenced to prison.

Pattern of crime:

Arson

Number of victims:

Fifty-two people died in the fire and
dozens more were injured.

Chapter 6

Cyberterrorism:

DISRUPTING INFRASTRUCTURE

What if the nation's infrastructure—including its power facilities, transportation networks, and financial services industries—became the targets of a cyberattack? The simple answer is that the US government might not be able to function and a disruption of key public services that people rely on every day, from banking systems and ATM machines to electricity and power services and communication networks, could bring society to a sudden halt.

It's a concern our federal government is taking seriously. At the Summit on Cybersecurity and Consumer Protection in 2015, President Barak Obama addressed the government's concern over such an attack, saying, "Much of our critical infrastructure—our financial systems, our power grid, health systems—run on networks connected to the Internet, which is hugely empowering but also dangerous, and creates new points of vulnerability that we didn't have before. Foreign governments and criminals are probing these systems every single day. We only have to think of real-life examples—an air traffic control system going down and disrupting flights, or blackouts that plunge cities into darkness—to imagine what a set of systematic cyberattacks might do."[1]

What Is Cyberterrorism?

Cyberterrorism is a new form of twenty-first century terrorism designed around society's dependence on technology. We use technology for nearly everything we do: to communicate with one another, make large and small purchases, access medical records, manage our transportation systems, and conduct online banking. Cyberterrorism is the disturbance of these technology-based systems to interrupt the government's ability to function or to disrupt business-related activities. This type of terrorism isn't as high profile as other types of terrorist attacks, such as bombings or mass shootings. But unlike those acts of terror, which intimidate society at large but only directly affect the lives of the victims, cyberterrorism can affect potentially thousands of people by destroying the digital life of anyone whose personal information is stolen in a cyberattack.

The purpose of cyberterrorism is the theft of personal information and military secrets, the disruption of business operations, and the crippling of a nation's infrastructure. Cyberterrorism is costly to the organization that has been hacked, to the people whose personal information has been stolen, and to the government whose

President Barack Obama speaks during the 2015 White House Summit on Cybersecurity and Consumer Protection in Stanford, California.

secrets have been revealed. For a company, a cyber hack forces a business's operations to be disrupted. Employees must focus on what information has been stolen, mediate any damage, install new protective measures to thwart the use of sensitive information, and engage in recovery efforts to see if information that was stolen can be reclaimed. A cyberattack can cost an organization hundreds of millions of dollars, depending on the size of the hack. For the individual, personal information, such as social security numbers, bank account numbers, medical information, and other sensitive data, can be sold on the black market. This can mean credit cards and loans can be opened in someone else's name, and money can be stolen from banking institutions. And for a government, sensitive military and personnel secrets can be revealed, putting the nation at risk.

Cyberterrorists conduct their operations with little or no risk to themselves. Most of the time, these terrorists hide behind an organization and are not individually known to law enforcement agencies. This makes identifying and prosecuting a cyber criminal very difficult.

Each day, cyberterrorists attack computer networks in the hopes of obtaining sensitive information and personal data they can use in some malicious way. Computer networks are protected by sophisticated cyberdefense systems designed to detect, thwart, and report an attack or an attempted attack. Most of the time, these defense systems work and a cyberattack is foiled. But for those times when cyberattacks do succeed, they tend to succeed in a big way, resulting in massive breaches of security and the exposure of millions of pieces of sensitive and personal information.

Cyberterrorists sell the information they obtain on the dark web. According to PCAdvisor.com, the dark web refers to "a collection of websites that are publicly visible, but hide the IP addresses of the servers that run them."[2] Normally an IP, or Internet Protocol, address provides some basic information about the server housing the website, such as its geographic location and sometimes its owner. Anyone can visit these dark websites, if you can find them. Even though there are millions of dark websites, they do not show up on search engines and the website's owners hide their identity through encryption tools. The only way to get access is to download special software that enables you to gain access to the dark web.

Who Is Motivated to Hack?

Cyberterrorists can include a range of individuals, including hacktivists, cybercriminals, and cyberspies. Hacktivists are people who break into networks largely to disrupt them and make a political point. According to ComputerWorld.com, hacktivists, like all activists, can be forces of good or evil. Anonymous, a group of individuals that work together on socially relevant topics, are known to hack into the computer networks of government institutions, companies, and media organizations. While they have stolen sensitive information in the past and distributed it worldwide, the organization has been a source of good as well. Anonymous attacked ISIS, the terrorist organization responsible for a series of bombings and mass shootings in Paris, France, in November 2015. Anonymous hacked into and took down a number of ISIS-related Twitter accounts. They also revealed e-mail addresses and channels on Telegram, an encrypted-messaging app, that were being used by ISIS members to communicate with their members.[3] Disrupting ISIS's communication network helped to disable the terrorist organization.

Cybercriminals are those looking to commit fraud by hacking into financial institutions or retail companies in an attempt to steal personal banking information and credit card accounts. Cybercriminals hack into complex computer networks to steal this information to sell it on the black market.

Cyberspies are those who want to steal military secrets from an opposing government or a defense contractor to either learn secrets or to disrupt military operations.

Computer Hack of the US Office of Personnel Management

Chinese government, suspected hackers

In June 2015, the US Office of Personnel Management was hacked by the Chinese government. The OPM is responsible for managing security clearances for members of the federal government as well as a variety of employment and human resource functions, including background checks and financial information. When the hack was discovered, it revealed that the personal information of almost twenty-two million current and former federal employees had been stolen.[4] The information stolen included social security numbers, dates and places of birth, current and former addresses, and classified information pertaining to data uncovered by an employee's background check, such as information about an employee's spouse and friends, financial information, employment histories, criminal history, psychological records, and any past drug use.

A *Newsweek* article on the OPM network hack says that government-to-government cyberspying is considered fair game, and commonly done by most advanced nations, including the United States. This type of spying is done to keep nations accountable and to monitor

The US Office of Personnel Management in Washington, DC, was the victim of Chinese hackers who stole records of as many as twenty-two million government workers.

any potentially illegal or threatening activities that could cause harm to a country or its people.

With the advancement of cybersecurity technologies, the potential has been growing for the possibility of a major hack by those with an interest in countering cybersecurity efforts.

The exact date of the OPM cyberattack is unknown. What is known is how long it took investigators—roughly four months—to discover that information had been stolen. According to OPM, the breach was found after network administrators made upgrades to OPM's computer systems. However, it's the sale of this information on the black market that has the potential to be the most significant consequence of the hack. The stolen information could be used to blackmail federal employees. If this information was sold to a foreign government, the buyer would know who they could blackmail and for what. The data breach included not only personal information but might have also included a list of foreign contacts a federal employee has come into contact with. It's common for people in sensitive, high-security positions to provide a list of foreign contacts. If China discovered a list of its own citizens that have had undocumented contact with the United States, those Chinese nationals could be at risk of retaliation by their own government.[5] In addition to these national level security issues, identity theft and fraud are potential issues for each federal employee affected by the hack.

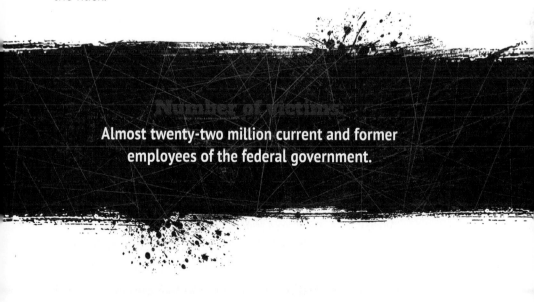

Number of victims:
Almost twenty-two million current and former employees of the federal government.

Computer Hack of Sony Pictures Entertainment

North Korean government, suspected hackers

The North Korean government is suspected of conducting a cyberattack on the computer systems of Sony Pictures Entertainment, a massive entertainment company that includes movie studios, television production companies, numerous music labels, and a media distribution unit. The company is behind the success of such movie franchises as Spiderman and James Bond.

In November 2015, Sony Pictures was preparing to release a movie titled *The Interview*, an action-comedy with a plot that included the assassination of North Korean leader Kim Jong Un. The North Korean government was enraged. In late November, when Sony employees logged onto their computers, a neon red skeleton appeared on their screens, along with a threat to publicly release massive amounts of data later that day.[6] The messages included links to download the data obtained in the hack, which included employee's medical information, social security numbers, e-mail correspondence, and performance evaluations. The information was not restricted to Sony's direct employees, but also included the personal information of many actors, actresses, and other celebrities that have appeared in movies, television productions, and other media projects.

Sony Pictures canceled the release of the film *The Interview* in response to the hack and to a potential threat made toward any theaters that showed the film.

The FBI was aware, through its connection to North Korean networks, that an attack on Sony Pictures was probable. According to a report, the National Security Association has hacked into North Korea's computer systems and planted beacons that reported information on North Korea's digital activities to the US government.[7]

Information obtained in the hack was also posted on WikiLeaks, which regularly publishes classified information and news leaks on its website. WikiLeaks published a searchable database of more

A poster for the comedy film *The Interview*

than thirty thousand documents from Sony Pictures, including 173,132 e-mails that revealed the company's business operations, as well as confidential e-mails that contained insensitive remarks about prominent actors and actresses in the entertainment industry. The social security numbers of nearly forty-seven thousand current or former Sony employees were also made public, including those of several actors and actresses.

Number of Victims

47,000 current and former employees of Sony Entertainment

Computer Hack of
Target Stores

Russian hackers suspected

It was the biggest retail hack to date and it occurred during the busiest time of the retail season: the holidays. Just prior to Thanksgiving in 2013, malware—intrusive or hostile software designed to cripple computer networks, spy on computer users, or steal information stored on computer systems—was installed in the security and payment systems used by Target and the company's eighteen hundred stores. The malware's mission was to capture and store every credit card number used during the holiday season. The information was stored on a Target server, which later was controlled by the hackers.[8]

Target investigated the hack after the US Department of Justice notified the retailer about the breach. In their investigation, Target found that alerts by their own cybersecurity program came on November 30, when hackers installed a first set of malware, and again on December 2, when hackers installed a second malware. The alerts notified Target before any of the information had been stolen, which means that, had Target responded, the outcome could have been different. As a result, the hackers successfully download

Holiday shopping at Target stores dropped by 46 percent the year following the computer hack.

the credit card numbers, addresses, phone numbers, and various other pieces of personal information from an estimated seventy million customers.

Like many businesses that rely on sophisticated computer systems to manage their day-to-day operations, Target had prepared for the possibility of a cyberattack. Just six months prior, the company bought and installed a malware detection tool by a cybersecurity firm called FireEye. Once embedded onto its computer system, FireEye was capable of detecting an attack. FireEye would notify Target's security specialists at the company's headquarters in Minneapolis, Minnesota. In this hacking instance, FireEye detected the illegal upload of malware designed to move the stolen information off the servers. The security team was informed immediately. However, nothing happened. The company did not respond to the alert.

According to IntelCrawler, a California-based cybersecurity firm, the mastermind behind the malware that captured Target's customer data was a seventeen-year-old Russian teenager, who sold his software to cybercriminals in Eastern Europe. Once the criminals began downloading data, the information was sent to several staging points in the United States, intended to mislead and cover the hackers' tracks. Before long, all of the information was sent to computers in Russia. The Target hack follows the pattern of cyberattacks on several other retail chains, including Neiman Marcus.

Customers and banks have filed more than ninety lawsuits against Target for its alleged negligence to respond to the cyberattack alerts. The lawsuits are in addition to other costs Target has endured. The company has spent millions of dollars to set up a customer-response operation and is offering free credit monitoring to catch any fraudulent charges that appear on customers' accounts. A year later, in 2015, Target reported that holiday shopping at its stores nationwide fell 46 percent compared to the same period a year before.

Number of victims:

An estimated seventy million credit card holders had their information stolen in the attack.

Computer Hack of Premera Blue Cross

Deep Panda, a Chinese hacking group, suspected

Premera Blue Cross, which provides health plans to people living in the Pacific Northwest, was hacked in May 2014 by a sophisticated breach that resulted in the theft of personal information of more than eleven million Premera customers.[9] Some of Premera's customers include those employed by major firms located in the region, including Amazon, Microsoft, and Starbucks.

Medical records are valuable for underground criminals, who use personal information to engage in insurance fraud. Because medical records include so much comprehensive personal information, including the results of medical tests and any procedures a patient has undergone, criminals are able to conduct in-depth medical fraud and make millions of dollars off of false claims to medical insurance companies. In the Premera hack, patients' names, dates of birth, social security numbers, mailing addresses, e-mail addresses, telephone numbers, member identification numbers, bank account information, insurance claim information, and clinical information were all obtained by the hackers.[10]

FBI Supervisory Special Agent J. Keith Mularski is the head of the cybercrime squad at the agency's Pittsburgh office. He is showing a screenshot from a dark website, a marketplace for cybercriminals and the largest-known English-speaking malware forum in the world. More than seventy alleged cybercriminals who have been using the website have been targeted by the US Department of Justice. They are suspected of buying and selling hacked databases, malicious software, and other products that cripple or steal information from computer systems.

Investigators believe the hack to be the work of Deep Panda, a Chinese espionage gang that cybersecurity experts know little about. Deep Panda was able to infiltrate Premera's computer system by creating fake websites that imitate Premera's corporate services.[11] Deep Panda is suspected of drawing customers to fake websites by sending out phishing e-mails. A phishing e-mail is a fraudulent message created to appear as if it has been sent from a legitimate organization or an individual known by the recipient. These e-mails often include a link that takes users to a fraudulent website that the user does not know is illegitimate. When a user logs in with his or her username and password, malware captures the log-in data and the hackers can use the information to access the company's real website and download its content.

Premera has spent millions to help its customers affected by the hack. The company set up a special telephone number and website. They have also warned customers to be aware of suspicious communications claiming to be from Premera Blue Cross, to monitor their insurance accounts for fraudulent claims, and to watch their credit activity for credit fraud. The company offered customers two years of credit monitoring for free.

The data of an estimated eleven million people has been obtained in the cyberattack.

CONCLUSION

Whether violence is associated with religious, pathological, issue-oriented, political, narcotics-based, or online terrorism, all acts of terrorism are designed to cause fear, intimidation, uncertainty, or death.

Terrorism, at its heart, is the physical, mental, and psychological anxiety created by acts of violence. Terrorism is a worldwide issue, and we're all effected by its reach— whether as victims or as observers of the events as they unfold on our television and computer screens. We watch in horror as innocent people are hurt and killed in the name of religion, politics, or for no purpose other than the sheer idea of terror itself. We're left to try to piece together reasons and explanations to help us understand the motives for such unnecessary violence.

Violent acts of terrorism—whether driven by a religious or political purpose, committed to draw attention to a cause or belief, an attempt to enact political change, an effort to influence a government, or to instill widespread fear, uncertainty, and intimidation—all produce feelings of sadness, pain, and confusion in the public. They also change the world as a whole and make people feel less safe no matter where they live or what their religious, political, or cultural beliefs.

Can Acts of Terrorism Be Prevented?

For religious terrorists groups, using violence is their way of influencing change and punishing those who do not hold their values. Preventing these acts has more to do with intelligence gathering on the part of a government, connecting the dots and thwarting an event before it happens. When it is an individual who wants to carry out terrorist activities, such as a bombing or mass shooting, recognizing the signs of mental illness or the clues that a person might be preparing to commit a terrorist attack could mean the difference between life and death for innocent people.

In the cases of mass murderers like Adam Lanza, Jared Lee Loughner, and Timothy McVeigh, individual signs of distress were likely evident in the months, weeks, and days leading up to the mass murders they committed. However, each sign, interpreted individually, might not have pointed to a call for help. Taken collectively, and within the context of their views on politics, religion, or in the presence of mental illness, these signs could have suggested that an event of some magnitude was imminent. If these individuals had been treated for mental illness, would the outcomes have been different? We will never know.

Introduction

1. Mark Roth, "Experts Track the Patterns of Mass Murders," *Pittsburgh Post-Gazette,* April 13, 2009, http://www.post-gazette.com/local/city/2009/04/13/Experts-track-the-patterns-of-mass-murders/stories/200904130098 (accessed March 2, 2016).
2. Hoffman, Bruce. *Inside Terrorism.* New York: Columbia University Press, 2006.

Chapter 1: Religious Terrorism: Killing for God and Country

1. "What happened on 9/11?" 911memorial.org, https://www.911memorial.org/faq-about-911 (accessed Dec. 10, 2015).
2. "Why did the terrorist attack the World Trade Center and the Pentagon?" 911memorial.org, https://www.911memorial.org/faq-about-911 (accessed Dec. 10, 2015).
3. Amy Zalman, PhD, "Religious Terrorism: A Short Primer on Religion and Terrorism," terrorism.about.com, http://terrorism.about.com/od/politicalislamterrorism/tp/Religious-terrorism.htm (accessed Dec. 10, 2015).
4. George Arnett, "Religious Extremism Main Cause of Terrorism, According to Report," *The Guardian*, http://www.theguardian.com/news/datablog/2014/nov/18/religious-extremism-main-cause-of-terrorism-according-to-report (accessed Dec. 10, 2015).
5. David Gibson, "Does Religion Cause Terrorism? It's Complicated," *Huffington Post*, http://www.huffingtonpost.com/2011/08/31/religion-terrorism_n_944143.html (accessed Dec. 10, 2015).
6. Tori DeAngelia, "Understanding Terrorism," apa.org, http://www.apa.org/monitor/2009/11/terrorism.aspx (accessed Dec. 18, 2015).
7. "2015 Global Peace Index," economicsandpeace.org, http://economicsandpeace.org/wp-content/uploads/2015/06/Global-Peace-Index-Report-2015_0.pdf (accessed Dec. 10, 2015).
8. Liah Greenfield, PhD, "Home-Grown Terrorists: Actually Terrorists or Mentally Ill?" psychologytoday.com, https://www.psychologytoday.

com/blog/the-modern-mind/201306/home-grown-terrorists-actually-terrorists-or-mentally-ill (accessed Jan. 8, 2016).

9. "Osama bin Laden: The Pan-Islamist Idea," history.com, http://www.history.com/topics/osama-bin-laden (accessed Dec. 10, 2015).

10. "1993 World Trade Center Bombing Fast Facts," CNN.com, http://www.cnn.com/2013/11/05/us/1993-world-trade-center-bombing-fast-facts/ (accessed Dec. 10, 2015).

11. "9/11: Timeline of Events," history.com, http://www.history.com/topics/9-11-timeline (accessed on Dec. 10, 2015).

12. Stephen A. Diamond, PhD, "On the violent life and death of Osama bin Laden: A psychological post-mortem," *psychologytoday.com*, https://www.psychologytoday.com/blog/evil-deeds/201105/the-violent-life-and-death-osama-bin-laden-psychological-post-mortem (accessed Dec. 10, 2015).

13. Lee Hancock, "Hasan forgoes statement on Fort Hood massacre," *Washington Post*, http://www.washingtonpost.com/wp-dyn/content/article/2010/11/15/AR2010111508320.html (accessed Dec. 10, 2015).

14. Nomaan Merchant and Paul J. Weber, "Fort Hood gunman meticulously planned attack," dallasnews.com, http://www.dallasnews.com/news/state/headlines/20130806-prosecutor-hasan-wanted-to-kill-many-soldiers.ece (accessed Dec. 10, 2015).

15. David Johnston and Scott Shane, "U.S. Knew of Suspect's Tie to Radical Cleric," *New York Times*, http://www.nytimes.com/2009/11/10/us/10inquire.html (accessed Dec. 10, 2015).

16. "Tim and Sarah Gayman Discuss Growing Up in Anti-Semitic Christian Identity Movement," splcenter.org, https://www.splcenter.org/fighting-hate/intelligence-report/2001/tim-and-sarah-gayman-discuss-growing-anti-semitic-christian-identity-movement?page=0%2C1 (accessed Dec. 10, 2015).

17. "Olympic Park Bomber Eric Rudolph Agrees to Plead Guilty," history.com, http://www.history.com/this-day-in-history/olympic-park-bomber-eric-rudolph-agrees-to-plead-guilty (accessed Dec. 10, 2015).

18. "Full Text of Eric Rudolph's Written Statements," armyofgod.com, http://www.armyofgod.com/EricRudolphStatement.html (accessed Dec. 10, 2015).

Chapter 2: Pathological Terrorism: Inflicting Fear and Terror

1. Steve Almasy, "In notebook read to jury, James Holmes wrote of 'obsession,'" CNN.com, http://www.cnn.com/2015/05/26/us/james-holmes-trial-notebook/ (accessed Dec. 18, 2015).

2. Nick Grothaus, "Types of Terrorism," handofreason.com, http://handofreason.com/2011/featured/types-of-terrorism (accessed Dec. 1, 2015).

3. Doug Saunders, "When troubled young men turn to terror, is it ideology or pathology?" globeandmail.com, http://www.theglobeandmail.com/news/national/lone-wolf-ideology-or-pathology/article21293910/ (accessed Jan. 8, 2016).

4. Stephen A. Diamond, PhD, "Anger, Rage and Pathological Embitterment: What Motivates Mass Murderers?" psychologytoday. com, https://www.psychologytoday.com/blog/evil-deeds/201110/anger-rage-and-pathological-embitterment-what-motivates-mass-murders (accessed Jan. 8, 2016).

5. Larry Greenemeier, "What Causes Someone to Act on Violent Impulses and Commit Murder?" scientificamerican.com, http://www.scientificamerican.com/article/anger-management-self-control/ (accessed Jan. 14, 2016).

6. Amanda Leigh Cowan, "Adam Lanza's Mental Problems 'Completely Untreated' Before Newtown Shootings, Report Says," *New York Times*, http://www.nytimes.com/2014/11/22/nyregion/before-newtown-shootings-adam-lanzas-mental-problems-completely-untreated-report-says.html?_r=0 (accessed Dec. 20, 2015).

7. "Adam Lanza Biography," biography.com, http://www.biography.com/people/adam-lanza-21068899#synopsis (accessed Dec. 23, 2015).

8. "Columbine High School Shooting," history.com, http://www.history.com/topics/columbine-high-school-shootings (accessed Dec. 9, 2015).

9. "Newly released Jared Lee Loughner files reveal chilling details," CBSnews.com, http://www.cbsnews.com/news/newly-released-jared-lee-loughner-files-reveal-chilling-details/ (accessed Jan. 8, 2016).

10. "The DC Sniper Beltway Attacks," crimemuseum.com, http://www.crimemuseum.org/crime-library/the-washington-dc-sniper (accessed Jan. 8, 2016).

Chapter 3: Issue-Oriented Terrorism: Killing for a Cause

1. David Staba, "Doctor's killer tries to make abortion the issue." *New York Times*, http://www.nytimes.com/2007/01/13/nyregion/13abort.html?_r=0 (accessed Jan. 8, 2016).

2. "Suspect tells newspaper he killed abortion doctor," *New York Times*, http://www.nytimes.com/2002/11/21/nyregion/suspect-tells-newspaper-he-killed-abortion-doctor.html (accessed Jan. 10, 2016).

3. Sivan Hirsch-Hoefler and Cas Mudde, "Ecoterrorism: Threat or political ploy?" *Washington Post*, https://www.washingtonpost.com/blogs/monkey-cage/wp/2014/12/19/ecoterrorism-threat-or-political-ploy/ (accessed Dec. 6, 2015).

4. "From decorated veteran to mass murderer: Oklahoma City Bomber a study in contradictions" CNN.com, www.cnn.com/CNN/Programs/people/shows/mcveigh/profile.html (accessed Jan. 6, 2016).

5. Elizabeth Mehren and John J. Goldman, "2 killed, 5 wounded at 2 abortion clinics. Gunman dressed in black opens fire in facilities near Boston; Extensive manhunt is launched. All the victims were employees or volunteers," latimes.com, http://articles.latimes.com/1994-12-31/news/mn-14945_1_abortion-clinic (accessed Jan. 4, 2016).

6. Christopher Daly, "Salvi convicted of murder in shootings," washingtonpost.com, http://www.washingtonpost.com/wp-srv/local/longterm/aron/salvi021996.htm (accessed Jan. 8, 2016).

7. James Brooke, "Group claims responsibility for blazes at Vail resort," *New York Times*, http://www.nytimes.com/1998/10/22/us/group-claims-responsibility-for-blazes-at-vail-resort.html (accessed on Dec. 10, 2015).

8. "Two plead guilty in 1998 arson of Vail ski resort; attack caused $12M in damage," *USA Today*, http://usatoday30.usatoday.com/news/nation/2006-12-14-vail-arsons_x.htm (accessed Dec. 22, 2015).

Chapter 4: Political Terrorism: Influencing Change Through Violence

1. Ed Payne, , "Emanuel African Methodist Episcopal: A storied church in a historic city," CNN.com, http://www.cnn.com/2015/06/18/us/charleston-emanuel-ame-church-history/ (accessed Jan. 5, 2016).

2. Clark Mindock, "Charleston Shooting Racial Motivation? Dylann Storm Roof Told Black Neighbor He Planned On Killing," ibtimes.com, http://www.ibtimes.com/charleston-shooting-racial-motivation-dylann-storm-roof-told-black-neighbor-he-1974050 (accessed Jan. 4, 2016).

3. "Profile: Wisconsin Sikh temple shooter Wade Michael Page," bbc.com, http://www.bbc.com/news/world-us-canada-19167324 (accessed Dec 10, 2015).

4. Erica Goode and Serge F. Kovaleski, "Wisconsin killer fed and was fueled by hate-driven music," *New York Times*, http://www.nytimes.com/2012/08/07/us/army-veteran-identified-as-suspect-in-wisconsin-shooting.html (accessed Dec. 10, 2015).

5. Joby Warrick, Marilyn W. Thompson, and Nelson Hernandez, "A Scientist's quiet life took a darker turn," *Washington Post*, http://www.washingtonpost.com/wp-dyn/content/article/2008/08/01/AR2008080102326.html (accessed Jan. 14, 2016).

6. "Timeline: How the Anthrax terror unfolded," npr.com, http://www.npr.org/2011/02/15/93170200/timeline-how-the-anthrax-terror-unfolded (accessed Jan. 14, 2016).

7. Joby Warrick, "FBI investigation of 2001 anthrax attacks concluded; U.S. releases details," *Washington Post*, http://www.washingtonpost.

com/wp-dyn/content/article/2010/02/19/AR2010021902369.
html?sid=ST2010021904257 (accessed Jan. 14, 2016).

Chapter 5: Narcotics-Based Terrorism: Killing for Control of the Drug Market

1. "United States Southern Command: About Us," southcom.mil, http://www.southcom.mil/aboutus/Pages/About-Us.aspx (accessed Jan. 14, 2016).
2. James Kitfield, "Confronting the nacroterrorism nexus," news.yahoo.com, http://news.yahoo.com/confronting-the-narcoterrorism-nexus-181859104.html (accessed Jan. 14, 2016).
3. "Drug trafficking and the financing of terrorism." UNODC.org, https://www.unodc.org/unodc/en/frontpage/drug-trafficking-and-the-financing-of-terrorism.html (accessed Jan. 14, 2016).
4. Alejandro Sanchez, "Pablo Escobar's legacy, 20 years later," *Huffington Post*, http://www.huffingtonpost.com/2013/12/02/pablo-escobar-death_n_4373016.html (accessed Jan. 14, 2016).
5. Fernando Ramos and Rafael Romo, "Colombia frees Escobar hitman who killed hundreds," CNN.com, http://www.cnn.com/2014/08/27/world/americas/colombia-hit-man-released/ (accessed Jan. 14, 2015).
6. "Spain Train Bombings Fast Facts," CNN.com, http://www.cnn.com/2013/11/04/world/europe/spain-train-bombings-fast-facts/ (accessed Jan. 14, 2016).
7. "Madrid bombers financed operation with drug sales, Spain says," *USA Today*, http://usatoday30.usatoday.com/news/world/2004-04-14-spain-attack-drugs_x.htm (accessed Jan. 14, 2016).
8. Nathanial Parish Flannery, "Monterrey, Mexico's Most 'Americanized City,' Charts a New Path Away from Violence," nearshoreamericas.com, http://www.nearshoreamericas.com/monterrey-mexicos-bustling-city-set-outshine-guadalajara/ (accessed Jan. 15, 2016).
9. Ioan Grillo, "Burning Down Casino Royale: Mexico's Latest Drug Atrocity," time.com, http://content.time.com/time/world/article/0,8599,2090601,00.html (accessed Jan. 15, 2016).

10. "Mexico Casino Massacre: Suspects Only Wanted to 'Scare' Owners," latino.foxnews.com, http://latino.foxnews.com/latino/news/2011/08/30/mexico-massacre-suspects-only-wanted-to-scare-casino-owners/ (accessed Jan. 15, 2016).

Chapter 6: Cyberterrorism: Disrupting Infrastructure

1. "Remarks by the President at the Cybersecurity and Consumer Protection Summit," whitehouse.gov, https://www.whitehouse.gov/the-press-office/2015/02/13/remarks-president-cybersecurity-and-consumer-protection-summit (accessed Jan. 14, 2016).
2. Matt Egan, "What Is the Dark Web? How to Access the Dark Web. What's the Difference between the Dark Web and the Deep Web?" pcadvisor.co.uk, http://www.pcadvisor.co.uk/how-to/internet/what-is-dark-web-how-access-dark-web-deep-joc-3593569/ (accessed Jan. 14, 2016).
3. Don Reisinger, "Anonymous Hacks Nissan Site to Support Whales." fortune.com, http://fortune.com/2016/01/14/anonymous-nissan-whales-hack/ (accessed Jan. 14, 2016).
4. Jonathan Broder, "Why the U.S. can't stop China's cyberspies." *Newsweek*, http://www.newsweek.com/2015/09/25/why-us-cant-stop-chinas-cyberspies-372890.html (accessed Jan. 8, 2016).
5. Kim Zetter, and Andy Greenberg, "Why the OPM breach is such a security and privacy debacle," wired.com, http://www.wired.com/2015/06/opm-breach-security-privacy-debacle/ (accessed Jan. 8, 2016).
6. Andrea Peterson, "The Sony Pictures hack, explained," *Washington Post*, https://www.washingtonpost.com/news/the-switch/wp/2014/12/18/the-sony-pictures-hack-explained/ (accessed Jan. 14, 2015).
7. Jamie Condliffe, "The NSA saw signs that the Sony hacks were coming," Gizmodo, http://gizmodo.com/the-nsa-saw-signs-that-the-sony-hacks-were-coming-1680362941 (accessed Jan. 14, 2016).
8. Michael Riley, Ben Elgin, Dune Lawrence and Carol Matlack, "Missed alarms and 40 million stolen credit card numbers: How Target blew it." Bloomberg, http://www.bloomberg.com/bw/articles/2014-03-13/target-missed-alarms-in-epic-hack-of-credit-card-data (accessed Jan. 14, 2015).

9. Julianne Pepitone, "Premera Blue Cross hacked: 11 million customers could be affected," nbcnews.com, http://www.nbcnews.com/tech/security/premera-blue-cross-hacked-11-million-customers-affected-n325231 (accessed Jan 14, 2016).

10. Jim Finkle, "Premera Blue Cross Hacked, Medical Information Of 11 Million Customers Exposed," *Huffington Post*, http://www.huffingtonpost.com/2015/03/17/premera-blue-cross-cybera_n_6890194.html (accessed Jan. 14, 2016).

11. Jeremy Kirk, "Premera, Anthem data breaches linked by similar hacking tactics," computerworold.com, http://www.computerworld.com/article/2898419/data-breach/premera-anthem-data-breaches-linked-by-similar-hacking-tactics.html (accessed Jan. 14, 2016).

Glossary

afterlife—Life after death.

antidote—A substance that counteracts some forms of poisoning.

appease—Bending to one's demands.

casualties—Deaths resulting from an event.

divine—Relating to God or a god, or coming from a god.

embitterment—The state of feeling bitterness or anger.

fugitive—Someone on the run from law enforcement.

grassroots—Generated or created by the common people; the most basic level of an organization.

ideology—A system of beliefs.

jihad—An Arabic word meaning "holy war."

magazine—An ammunition storage and feeding device used in some firearms.

mainstream—A leading or prevailing thought among many.

malware—Software intended to cause damage to computer networks and files.

microbiology—The study of very small biologic organisms.

pan-Islamist—A political movement promoting unity among all Muslims; Muslims under one Islamic state.

petty crime—Minor crime, such as shoplifting or trespassing.

psychopathy—A generalized term meaning mental illness or disorder.

resentment—Feelings of anger for being treated differently of unfairly.

Sharia—The Islamic legal system.

Books

Brown, Don. *America Is Under Attack: September 11, 2001: The Day the Towers Fell.* New York: Square Fish Books, 2014.

Felix, Rebecca, and Matthew McCabe. *12 Things to Know About Terrorism.* St. Paul, MN: Black Rabbit Books, 2015.

Green, Robert. *Global Perspectives: Terrorism.* North Mankato, MN: Cherry Lake Publishing, 2014.

Marlowe, Christie. *Terrorism and Perceived Terrorist Threats.* Broomall, PA: Mason Crest, 2015.

Websites

911memorial.org

The 911memorial.org website is the official online presence of the National September 11 Memorial Museum at the World Trade Center. The website provides information about the events of 9/11, as well as an educational section with teaching guidelines designed for parents and teachers to discuss the 9/11 terrorist attacks.

FBI Kids

fbi.gov/fun-games/kids

The FBI Kids website is an interactive way for elementary, middle, and high school students to learn more about the activities, mission, and purpose of the FBI.

Films

Al-Qaeda's New Front. Neil Docherty. PBS, 2005.

State of Fear: The Truth About Terrorism. Pamela Yates. Skylight Pictures, 2005.

Index